Demystifying Differentiation in Middle School

Tools, Strategies, and Activities to Use NOW

Caroline C. Eidson
Robert Iseminger
Chris Taibbi

Pieces of Learning

CLC0410
ISBN 978-1-931334-99-0
© 2007 Pieces of Learning
www.piecesoflearning.com
www.differentiatedresources.com
Printed by Total Printing Systems, Newton, IL
09/2010

Demystifying Differentiation in Middle School
Tools, Strategies, and Activities to Use NOW

Introduction	The What and Why	5
	The Who	5
	The How	6
Chapter 1	What is Differentiation and Why Should We Be Doing It?	9
	A Quick Look at the Basics of Differentiation	10
	The Rationale Behind Differentiation	12
Chapter 2	Tools for Differentiating Instruction	13
Chapter 3	Strategies for Differentiating Instruction	19
Chapter 4	Language Arts	29
Chapter 5	Math	57
Chapter 6	Science	82
Chapter 7	Social Studies	109
Chapter 8	Assessing Learning in a Differentiated Classroom	137
	Resources	144

Dedication:

We dedicate this book to all the teachers with whom we have worked on this essential, and oft times challenging, approach to teaching known as "differentiation."

Their willingness to reflect on their own teaching, to explore new instructional methods, and to work toward challenge and success for their students has helped us to stretch our own perceptions of what education *should* and *can* be.

It is indeed an honor, a privilege, and an inspiration to be part of the lives of such committed professionals.

Introduction

The What and Why

Our work as teachers and educational consultants has given us the opportunity to meet many K through12 educators across the country, and it is with these people in mind that we first conceived this book. As the three of us began sharing stories with one another about our interactions with different groups of teachers, we discovered an almost constant refrain we hear from teachers as we share examples of different strategies that support differentiation: *"Where can I find a book that has a bunch of these kinds of activities that I can use in my classroom?"* We also found that our responses to that question were strikingly similar: *"There are a few focused on the elementary level, but none that we know of for middle school and high school."*

While there are many books available about curriculum differentiation, most of them address the theory and rationale behind it and discuss models and strategies that support it. Some of these books offer limited examples of differentiated tasks and activities. However, none provide a comprehensive collection of activities that demonstrate how differentiation can be used in different subject areas at the middle and high school levels.

So we wrote this book with the teachers we have worked with in mind. We thought about what they might really want and need as they work to meet their students' needs. We settled on a book for middle school teachers because in our work they have been the most vocal about wanting resources that provide examples of differentiated activities and tasks.

The Who

Of course, this book is for all middle school teachers and administrators who are looking for ways to make curriculum differentiation work in their classrooms.

But in writing this book, we made a few assumptions about our audience. Because we did not want to create another book about the basics of and rationale for differentiation (though we discuss these briefly in Chapter 1), we first assumed that teachers reading this book would have some background with differentiation, perhaps through coursework, workshops, or through reading and research. We also assumed that they would buy into the idea of differentiation, that they would realize the time and effort that it can require can mean greater learning for students and would also believe that it is a valuable tool for meeting student needs in mixed-ability settings. We then assumed that our readers would believe in the need for high expectations for all learners and would be striving to challenge all students. With these assumptions in mind, we wrote this book for teachers and administrators who are ready to take differentiation to the next level in their classrooms and schools, who believe that differentiation works, and who are looking for more examples of it.

The How

Any author who writes about instructional practices and strategies hopes that educators will take what is written on the page and will adapt it to meet their own needs and situations. And so it is with us. While we expect that teachers will use many of the activities and tasks just as we present them in this book, it is our hope that they will also use them as jumping-off points for creating their own differentiated lessons. Thus, we hope that this book empowers teachers first by doing much of the work of differentiation for them and second by encouraging through example the design and use of other differentiated activities and tasks.

To this end, we have provided background information for each activity presented. This information includes a brief overview addressing any instructional or management issues related to the activity, standards, and objectives addressed, and the basis for the differentiation provided.

Because we want teachers to adapt the activities as needed for the classes and grades they teach, we have not designated specific grades for them. Rather, we have offered a range of activities and topics in each subject area that are representative of middle school standards and objectives in various states. It is our hope that this approach will provide teachers and administrators with the flexibility either to use the differentiated activities as they are presented or to create their own using the tools and techniques provided in this book.

We wrote this book for teachers and administrators who are ready to take differentiation to the next level in their classrooms and schools, who believe that differentiation works, and who are looking for more examples of it.

Differentiation does not mean that all students receive the same instruction, materials, and tasks. It means they receive the instruction, materials, and tasks they need to maximize their learning.

© **Pieces of Learning**

Chapter 1: What is Differentiation and Why Should We Be Doing It?

Our job as teachers in differentiated classrooms is like that of a coach. We have "players" who come to us with different skills, talents, and interests. It is the team we are given, and we must "win" with this team by making every player the best he can be and by finding where each one fits in our master plan for success. We must organize practices and activities that prepare each player for "game day." In the classroom that may be the "big test," but as any good coach knows, the real game is life. The experience students have in our classrooms should leave them not only with a better knowledge of our subject area, but also with information about themselves that they can use to be successful in other areas of school and in life.
- Social Studies teacher, North Carolina

There are many ways of going forward, but only one way of standing still.
- Franklin D. Roosevelt

Thinking about athletics is an apt place to begin building an understanding of and rationale for curriculum differentiation. Certainly a soccer coach spends a vast amount of time and energy learning about her players' skills in order to design a winning team. Players are matched to field positions that highlight their strengths and downplay their weaknesses. And yet, throughout the season, it is the coach's job to ensure that every player's skills improve. Through well-thought-out practices and drills and hard-won (or lost) games, players come to understand the strategy behind the sport and build on the skills they brought to the field on the first day of practice. This is true for the stars of the team as well as for the benchwarmers.

So let's apply this approach to our classrooms. What would classrooms look like if teachers were able to determine their students' skills and talents early in the year, continue to assess students' growth in an on-going manner throughout the year, and then match students to learning tasks designed to further improve their skills and talents? What would classrooms look like if they focused on growth for all students regardless of their starting points? The answer:

What is Differentiation?

They would look like differentiated classrooms.

This chapter provides an overview of curriculum differentiation rather than an in-depth exploration of it. There has been much attention paid to this topic in recent years, and for those seeking more information about differentiation, we recommend the many works of Carol Ann Tomlinson (see the Resource List provided at the end of the book).

A Quick Look at the Basics of Differentiation

Differentiation occurs when teachers take proactive steps to meet students' varied needs in the classroom. It is tempting to look at students' needs in terms of ability only, but in a differentiated classroom, the teacher understands that students bring much more to the environment than just what they already know or are capable of picking up quickly. They also bring different learning styles and interests.

Teachers in differentiated classrooms use as much information as they can about their students to design curriculum and instruction that provides both success and challenge for all. So, for example, while studying the Middle Ages, what would students be interested in learning more about, either individually or in small groups? Do some students benefit more from working in pairs or groups while others are at their best when working on their own? And of course, how can students who already grasp much of the material being presented go further in their understanding, while other students can get the more basic information that they need?

In terms of what can be differentiated in a classroom, if a teacher can design it, it can be differentiated. A simple way to look at what can be differentiated is through content, process, and product. Certainly a teacher can differentiate what students will learn (content) by addressing different learning objectives, by focusing on concepts and generalizations that encourage different levels of understanding, and by providing a range of materials and resources. Likewise, almost every learning objective has multiple ways that students can achieve it (process). So, for instance, some students can come to understand a topic by reading various articles about it, while others can look at pictures or photographs related to it and draw their own conclusions, and still others can listen to music related to that same topic. Differentiating process asks teachers to provide a variety of different ways that students can make sense of a question, issue, or topic, or develop a skill.

Finally, teachers who differentiate products look for many ways for students to show or explain what they have learned. For example, these teachers allow students to choose from a list of product options when completing independent studies or small group investigations. They allow students to respond to information in different formats so that some students can write about their understandings while others can diagram or illustrate theirs. These teachers might even differentiate unit tests and quizzes, asking different questions depending on students' experiences and levels of growth throughout a unit.

The foundation for effective differentiation is clarity about what students should gain from a particular unit of study. Whether differentiating or not, it is a lot easier for a teacher to design constructive lessons and assessments and to measure student growth when he knows ahead of time what his learning objectives are. So before beginning to differentiate instruction in a particular unit, teachers must establish their objectives for that unit. And once the unit has begun, they must keep their "eye on the ball" – objectives – by making sure that the resources they are providing and the tasks they are assigning directly address their objectives.

Once teachers select or design the learning objectives, assessment begins and becomes the basis for decisions about what students need. It should be ongoing and varied, providing current information about students' progress. Look for more on the important role of assessment in Chapter 8.

The cycle of assessment and learning in a differentiated classroom provides both success and challenge for all learners so that all come to feel they are working hard and their hard work is paying off. No student should be made to feel incapable or unworthy because he lacks some prerequisites. Likewise, no

What is Differentiation?

student should find that his days are filled with busywork that requires little effort. Differentiation ensures that teaching is responsive to learners' needs and provides a framework for helping teachers take their learners as far as they can go as quickly as they can move.

The Rationale Behind Differentiation

Teaching is difficult. This is true whether you are teaching five-year-olds how to tie their shoes or twelve-year-olds how to balance equations. And certainly it is the case that differentiating curriculum and instruction places additional demands on teachers' time and energy. But when learning is at stake, it is hard to argue against an approach that benefits our students and ensures growth for all. Just as a doctor would never prescribe the same medication to all of his patients regardless of their differing symptoms, teachers seeking to meet their students' learning needs cannot expect that all will benefit from the same teaching.

Differentiation asks us to redefine what "fair" is in our classrooms. Does it mean that all students receive the same instruction, materials, and tasks? Or does it mean that all students receive the instruction, materials, and tasks that they need in order to maximize their learning? Those in favor of differentiation argue that it means the latter, that it is, in fact, highly unfair to teach in a "one size fits all" mode.

From a teacher perspective, once the management piece has been tackled and the basics have been grasped and practiced, differentiation can be both exciting and challenging. It tests our creativity and asks us to look at our work more critically as we evaluate our attempts to meet our students' needs. It creates a dynamic learning environment where the daily routine is driven not by a textbook or a pacing guide but by the needs and interests of the learners. The results can be exhilarating.

Is it more work? Yes. Is it worth it? Absolutely.

Chapter 2: Tools for Differentiating Instruction

Our Age of Anxiety is, in great part, the result of trying to do today's job with yesterday's tools.

- Marshall McLuhan

Spoon feeding in the long run teaches us nothing but the shape of the spoon.

- E.M. Forster

The tools that teachers have at their disposal in today's classrooms are much richer than the ones we recall our teachers using during our own schooling. We now know significantly more about the brain and how it works than we did just 20 years ago, and this increase in knowledge is producing new educational models and approaches at almost lightning speed. While these new trends may be exciting, with so many new ideas and directions to choose from, teachers often feel the stress of being asked to implement too many initiatives coming at any one given time. How can we possibly know which will really be effective and which are practical in the "real world?"

In this chapter we focus on several models or "tools" that we have found to be most useful in our work with students and with teachers. While there are certainly numerous other tools available, we believe those we present here have stood the test of time and have proven to be "doable" for most teachers. What follows is only a brief introduction to each tool, and we hope that you will seek to learn more about them as your students' needs dictate.

Tools for Differentiating Based on Student Readiness

When we work with teachers who are looking for ways to address a range of readiness levels in their classrooms, we often recommend that they consider using the following tools to guide them through lesson design: Bloom's Taxonomy (either the old or new version),

Tools for Differentiating

Tomlinson's *Equalizer,* and concept-based teaching.

Most teachers are familiar with Bloom's Taxonomy as it has been a staple of teacher education programs for over 40 years. Originally designed as a means for identifying the degree of abstraction of questions that are typically asked in educational settings, this hierarchical model of thinking is now widely used to assist in the design of assignments and tasks that address different levels of readiness. Whether using the original version of the Taxonomy or the newer one, it is important to keep in mind that Bloom did not intend for his model to be used as a means for labeling students. That is, we should not consider some students to generally be "knowledge-level learners" while others might be labeled "synthesis and evaluation learners." Rather, we should keep in mind that there are times when even our most struggling thinkers are capable of thinking at higher levels. Similarly, there are certainly times when our most gifted learners must focus on basic recall of information, or lower-level thinking.

Bloom's Taxonomy can be applied to almost anything teachers create: for example, discussion questions, homework assignments, items for tests, and projects. The trick in using this thinking structure, as with any instructional tool, is to make sure to offer students adequate and appropriate challenges. This means that we focus on students working at as high a level of thinking as possible given their readiness with regard to the content being studied.

Tomlinson's *Equalizer* is a tool that asks teachers to consider how to modify lessons and student work across nine different dimensions. These dimensions include:

➢ Foundational to transformational
➢ Concrete to abstract
➢ Simple to complex
➢ Fewer facets to multi-facets
➢ Smaller leap to greater leap
➢ More structured to more open
➢ Clearly-defined problems to fuzzy problems
➢ Less independence to greater independence
➢ Slower pace to quicker pace

(From Carol Ann Tomlinson's *The Differentiated Classroom: Responding to the Needs of All Learners*, 1999)

Clearly, the great benefit of this tool is that it helps teachers think about ways to differentiate classroom learning across a wide range of student learning differences and needs. Rather than simply asking us to think in terms of "high ability" and "low ability," it addresses characteristics of learners that might be related as much to learning profile as to readiness. For example, we can certainly modify the amount of independence with which students are asked to work in a given assignment. We can also provide some students with a great deal of open-endedness in a given task while others might require a significantly greater degree of structure. In terms of readiness differences, some students may need to work with more concrete and simple resources and ideas while others may be ready to grapple with more abstraction and complexity.

Tomlinson's *Equalizer* works much like the knobs on a sound system's equalizer. By moving a knob from one end of the sound spectrum to the other, the quality of the music being produced can be modified. Likewise, a teacher using Tomlinson's *Equalizer* can move a knob anywhere along a given continuum to meet the needs of students during any given lesson or with a particular task. Tomlinson's *Equalizer* reminds us that there are many ways to think about differences in student readiness and there also are many possible approaches to responding to those differences.

Concept-based teaching directly addresses two of the dimensions on Tomlinson's *Equalizer* – concrete to abstract and simple to complex. During the planning process, it asks teachers to think about the "forest" rather than the "trees." When using this approach to instructional design, teachers focus on large (perhaps even huge) ideas and the generalizations, or big statements, that can be made about them. For example, a unit in history might become a study of *conflict* and *power* rather than simply a march through time. What can be said about the causes and effects of *conflict*? Why do people seek *power*? What is the relationship between *conflict* and *power*?

When we ask students to think about abstract ideas or concepts, we require them to think at a higher level and encourage them to make connections across time and disciplines. In addition to *conflict* and *power*, some useful concepts that apply to many subject areas and topics include (and this is just a short list of the many possibilities): change, patterns, exploration, communication, adaptation, systems, interdependence, wants and needs, survival, responsibility, courage, progress, growth, cycles, influence, and equality.

Tools for Differentiating Based on a Student Learning Profile

One of the easiest ways to address differing learning profiles in a classroom is to provide variety in the environment and in the grouping arrangements. What this may mean is that there are times when the room is silent, benefiting those who work best in silence, and there are other times when some noise is permitted, benefiting those who need some background sounds to do their best work. It may also mean that there are a variety of work spaces available to students. Some students may need isolated or clean and organized work areas, while others who may be able to handle some nearby activity or clutter.

It is certainly the case that some of us do our best work on our own and prefer to work that way, while others work best with a partner or in a group. In differentiated classrooms, teachers vary student groupings and often allow students to choose their own grouping configurations. Simply allowing students to work alone or with others when they want can mean the difference between a task that is finished only adequately and a job that is done well.

Another effective and frequently used tool for addressing learning profile differences is Gardner's Multiple Intelligences. Gardner originally conceived of seven different intelligences – verbal/linguistic, mathematical/logical, visual/spatial, musical, kinesthetic, interpersonal, and intrapersonal – and has since added an eighth, the naturalist. With many publications supporting his ideas, Gardner's model has become wildly popular in schools. Certainly, it is a fairly simple one to understand and apply, and by using it, a teacher is sure to be providing more variety in her teaching. This model is an effective and practical means for creating different tasks and product options.

Our intent with this chapter was to re-visit some lesson-design tools that teachers find useful when differentiating their instruction. There are thousands of teacher resources and websites available that probe more deeply the rationale for and implementation of these tools and that discuss other possible tools as well. It is important to note that the models and approaches presented here are those that we have applied in the sample activities and tasks presented in Chapters 4 through 7. They also complement the specific strategies presented in Chapter 3.

Keep in mind that, regardless of the tools that a teacher chooses to use, the goal in any classroom, differentiated or not, ought to be to aim high so that each and every student experiences an appropriate challenge. Given the fact that our students enter our classrooms with vastly different needs and readiness levels for learning, aiming high for all cannot mean the same instruction and work for all. This is, of course, why differentiation is a necessity in any classroom.

There are times when even our most struggling thinkers are capable of thinking at higher levels.

Regardless of the tools
that a teacher chooses to use,
the goal in any classroom, differentiated or not,
ought to be to aim high
so that each and every student
experiences an appropriate challenge.

Chapter 3: Strategies for Differentiating Instruction

It is a fundamental truth that children need well-educated teachers who are eclectic in their methods and willing to use different strategies, depending on what works best for which children.

Diane Ravitch
<u>*Left Back: A Century of Failed School Reforms*</u>

Variety is the spice of life.

Unknown

No one book could ever encompass all there is to know and learn about curriculum differentiation. And because differentiation really is more of a philosophy and approach to teaching than a collection of prescribed strategies, it is up to individual teachers to decide just how differentiation will look in their classrooms. It would be wonderful if one could go to a teacher supply store and purchase a kit for differentiating. Realistically, though, in any given classroom, that kit would not be tremendously responsive to students' needs. It is impossible for a teacher to predict ahead of time what those needs might be in a particular group. So it becomes each teacher's job to create his own "bag of tricks" for differentiating instruction.

We have found that, after many hours of discussing, modeling, and practicing differentiation with a particular group of teachers, each and every teacher leaves our time together with a different plan of action and with different goals for differentiating. That being said, we have chosen to focus on four strategies – **Tiered assignments, RAFT activities**, **Think-Tac-Toes**, and **Complex Instruction** – that most teachers find useful. They also want more examples of these strategies for use in their own classrooms. It may be helpful to flip back to some of the examples provided in the subject area chapters as you read about each of these strategies. We recognize that we could have included many more strategies, and we hope that you will continue your own search to learn more about strategies that support differentiation (see the Resource List provided at the end of the book).

Tiered Assignments

Also known as tiering and tiered instruction, tiered assignments are often the first strategy that teachers learn about as they begin their work with differentiation. It is difficult to imagine a differentiated classroom that does not, at some point, include tiered assignments. In fact, teachers who are unfamiliar with differentiation are often under the mistaken impression that tiered assignments are all there is to it.

Tiered assignments are based on student readiness and result in students either working together in small groups, in pairs, or individually to complete tasks that are based on their readiness levels. This means that teachers using tiered assignments first identify the objectives they need to teach and then find a way to assess students' current grasp of those objectives. Most often teachers know, either from their prior experiences with teaching specific content or from discovering through both formal and informal measures, that their students do not grasp and understand the same amount of material. Teachers also recognize that students have developed different skill sets, either in or out of school, and that they are at different points in terms of conceptual development. Once teachers recognize these kinds of differences in readiness, tiered assignments become a necessity.

We tend to think in terms of three groups or three different assignments when tiering:

- an assignment for students who are lacking a good deal of prior knowledge and experience with regard to the objectives
- an assignment for students who have mastered all of the objectives or can do so quickly
- an assignment for those who fall somewhere in between

There are certainly times, though, when two tiers are sufficient for meeting students' needs, and there are other times when a group of students may require more than three tiers.

It is tempting to put students into groups that ultimately remain fairly static. However, teachers in differentiated classrooms recognize that a student's readiness can change, sometimes very rapidly. One day a student can be lagging behind with regard to specific content or objectives, but the next day that same student might be ready to make a leap of some sort. At the middle school level, it can be dangerous to underestimate the role of hormones and social issues in the readiness of students. So teachers in differentiated classrooms take a flexible approach to assigning tasks to students. They understand that on any given day they may have to rethink the assignment they have planned for a particular student or group of students.

Because tiered assignments are based on student readiness and result in different levels of activities, teachers choose which assignment each student will complete. It would be nice if each student in a middle school classroom would, when given assignment options ranging in difficulty, select the option

that is appropriately challenging for her. But as all teachers know, students do not always make the best choices, and many will seek the "easy" way out. There are many times in a differentiated classroom when students ought to be given choices. It is just not wise to give them those choices when differentiating based on readiness.

Typically, teachers go through the following steps when tiering an assignment or activity:

1. **Identify the objectives to be tiered.** It is important to keep in mind that if the objectives are those that all students have already mastered then there is no reason to teach them directly. If they are objectives that no students in a class have mastered, then tiering may not be necessary, and whole group instruction may be preferable.

2. **Pre-assess students' grasp of the objectives.** Pre-assessment can take many forms, formal or informal. The trick here is to make sure that your pre-assessment is clearly aligned with your objectives. An assessment is

of little use if it does not tell us what we need to know about a student's knowledge, understanding, and skill level.

3. **Design or find one activity that addresses the objectives.** This activity is the basis for the other "tiers," so it should be a good one. This means that it should clearly address the objectives, that is should be age-appropriate and respectful of students' abilities, and that it should be engaging. It is a good idea to aim to the middle or high groups with this first activity as that will help ensure your expectations for all your tiers will be high. Starting the planning process with the lowest tier in mind often results in low expectations for all tiers.

4. **Design or find other tiers as needed.** As mentioned previously, there is no rule about the number of tiers a teacher should provide. Some content and classes might require only two tiers while others might require four or perhaps even five. If you are just starting out with differentiation,

we recommend beginning with fewer groups and working your way up to more as needed.

5. **Assign students to the appropriate tiered assignment.** At this point, it helps to have spent time analyzing the students' pre-assessments to determine which assignments will provide both challenge and success to which students. Are there some students who "aced" the pre-assessment while others struggled to complete most of the items on it? Which items are students missing? Time spent reflecting on the students' prior knowledge will help enormously when it is time to decide who does which tiered assignment. In terms of actually giving the appropriate assignments to students, we do not advise passing out all of the assignments to all of the students. This draws unnecessary attention to the fact that students will be completing different tasks. It is a good idea to give students only the assignments they will be responsible for completing.

6. **Be ready to make changes.** There is no accounting for changes, sometimes rapid, in students' readiness for learning, so it is a good idea to be flexible when assigning tiered activities.

Tiered assignments are ultimately the backbone of the differentiated classroom. They allow teachers to respond to the fact that some students enter our classrooms with vast amounts of prior knowledge while others are sorely lacking in information and skills. And yet, we need to find a way to challenge them all.

RAFT Activities

RAFT activities can be great fun to design and complete. Once teachers learn this strategy, they often find themselves using it again and again. RAFT is an acronym for ROLE, AUDIENCE, FORMAT, and TOPIC. When designing these activities, teachers must consider the roles they want their students to assume, the audiences that students should address, the formats (most often written) that students' work can take, and the topics students must respond to. As with tiered assignments, when designing RAFT activities, teachers should first be clear about their objectives.

The great thing about RAFT activities is that they allow for a great deal of creativity, for both teachers and students, while providing many avenues for differentiation. A teacher might want to address student readiness differences by differentiating the abstractness of the role students will take on or the complexity or open-endedness of the topic they will address. On the other hand, she might choose to respond to learning profile differences in her classroom by offering a variety of different formats for students' products. For example, a letter or speech draws on verbal/linguistic intelligence while a top ten list or time line draws on mathematical/ logical skills. RAFT assignments can also be used as part of other strategies for differentiation. For instance, they can be used as tiered assignments and as options on Think-Tac-Toes or as Complex Instruction tasks.

RAFT activities can be used in all subject areas and at all grade levels to encourage students to apply and analyze information and understandings that they have mastered or are mastering. And these activities can be either teacher assigned or student selected depending on how they are differentiated. It is important to keep in mind that when RAFT activities are differentiated based on student readiness they should be assigned by the teacher. However, students can certainly be allowed to choose the activity they want to work on when the activities have been differentiated based on student learning profile or interest. Probably the most difficult part of creating effective RAFT activities is ensuring that they are linked to previously identified objectives. However, this challenge is outweighed by the fact that teachers often enjoy creating these highly engaging activities.

Think-Tac-Toes

Of all the strategies we share with teachers, Think-Tac-Toes usually spark the greatest interest. While tiered assignments are fundamental to a differentiated classroom and allow for a great deal of teacher "control," many teachers seem most drawn to Think-Tac-Toes. Moreover, students like them, too, because they provide students with a great deal of choice. Think-Tac-Toes are a form of learning contracts. When designed well, they invite students to work in ways that are based on their learning profiles and interests and that focus on important knowledge, understandings, and skills. They make very effective assessments at the end of a unit, and teachers often use them in addition to more formal assessments.

Typically, Think-Tac-Toes are created in 3 x 3 grids, providing nine possible tasks. Students select a given number of tasks to complete, but completing three tasks is generally the goal. It is up to the teacher to decide if students need to connect the tasks in rows, columns, or diagonally. A great way to "tighten up" a Think-Tac-Toe is to make each row focus on a particular objective or aspect of the content, and then ask students to choose a task from each row.

Because students make choices based on their learning profiles and interests in the tasks to be completed on a Think-Tac-Toe, it is important to keep the readiness levels of the tasks fairly similar. If students find that some tasks appear more simple than others, they may choose those tasks and avoid more challenging tasks that might be more appropriate for them. Teachers who want to address readiness while using Think-Tac-Toes should be prepared to tier them, thus creating two or more Think-Tac-Toes and then assigning the appropriate ones to the students who need them (see the Tiered Literature Think-Tac-Toes provided in Chapter 4). This allows teachers to provide students with choice while ensuring they are being adequately challenged. As with any strategy for differentiation, it is important to maintain focus on the objectives – something that can be difficult to do during the process of creating a variety of tasks.

Complex Instruction

Complex Instruction is aptly named. Usually when we share this strategy with a group of teachers, we ask them to put down their pencils and just listen the first time through. However, once they "get it," it becomes a favorite. Complex Instruction provides an effective and sensible answer to the question of how to group students in mixed-readiness groups while ensuring a meaningful learning experience for all involved. So often when teachers mix abilities in their groupings they find that some students end up completing the lion's share of the work while others sit back and watch.

As with all instruction, the starting point for Complex Instruction is the learning objectives to be addressed. Once a teacher has determined those, he then reflects on his students and notes the strengths they have. Are some learners highly creative, divergent thinkers? Are others natural actors? Skilled researchers? Talented artists? When considering the strengths of a group of students, the sky is almost the limit.

Once the strengths have been identified, the teacher then creates mixed-strength groups. So, for instance, if he decides that he has many creative thinkers, researchers, writers, illustrators, and speakers and dramatists, he creates small groups comprised of students who have each of these five talents. Thus, each group will have a creative thinker, a researcher, a writer, an illustrator, and a speaker. Of course, classes rarely provide opportunity for equally numbered groups, so some groups may lack a person representing a specific talent.

At this point, the teacher is ready to design the tasks that will be carried out by each small, mixed-strength group. He reflects on his objectives and creates a task for each of the talents represented in the small groups. Thus, there should be a task appropriate for a creative thinker, one for a researcher, and so forth. In this case, he will design five tasks. These tasks will then be distributed in writing to each small group, and the students will spend time deciding who will take the lead on each task.

In our experience, students usually gravitate toward the task that has been designed with their strength or talent in mind. On occasion, however, a teacher might have to consult with a group of students to help them decide who will do which tasks.

In terms of logistics, it is important to give each small group the same number of tasks as there are group members. Thus, no groups end up having more tasks than they have someone to tackle

them. At times, it is beneficial for students in the small groups to work together to complete a task or two. This sort of collaboration should be encouraged. In addition, it helps to tell the students that they will be evaluated both individually and as a group. Then no one is penalized because others are not focusing on their tasks.

Complex Instruction takes time to plan, but the pay off is sizeable. When it is done well, it leads to some interesting collaborations and causes students to create a variety of products that are based on their strengths. Time and time again, we find this to be a highly effective strategy in a differentiated classroom and a welcome alternative to cooperative grouping.

Some Final Thoughts

Some strategies for differentiating instruction take longer to plan and prepare than others. For instance, RAFT activities can be fairly simple to create because there is a prescribed format for doing so, while creating Think-Tac-Toes and Complex Instruction tends to take much more effort and time. It is typical, though, for students to spend a longer amount of time working on Think-Tac-Toe and Complex Instruction tasks than on RAFT activities. And while it might take some time to create tiered projects, designing tiered writing prompts may take much less time. Again, differentiated instruction will look different in every classroom where it is used.

Effective classroom management is crucial in any classroom, but it takes on even more importance in a differentiated classroom where students are often expected to take responsibility for their own learning. It is easy to understate the need for practice of routines in a differentiated classroom, but that practice is often the difference between a classroom where differentiation runs smoothly and one where it does not. Students must be able to move quickly from one place in the classroom to another (a kitchen timer works wonders), and they need to know where to place completed work, where to place unfinished work, and where to find the materials necessary for task completion.

Another important management consideration focuses on keeping students engaged, even when the teacher is not working with them, and they are not sure what they should be doing. There are times in all classrooms when students finish work and assessments early or come to a point in their work where they can go no further without assistance from the teacher. Teachers in differentiated classrooms use **anchor activities** to ensure that student engagement continues despite these issues. These activities are also useful when a teacher needs to present a task to one group before interacting with other groups. While she works with one group to get them started on their assignments, the rest of the students can be engaged with anchor activities.

Anchor activities are tasks that students can do and will do on their own. Silent reading can be a great anchor activity, but only for those students who enjoy reading. For those who do not, it can be an enormous chore and is not likely to keep them engaged. Many teachers post a list of possible anchor activities so that students have some choice in the tasks they will complete on their own. Effective anchor activities focus on important skills and are not busywork. They can relate to a specific unit or they can be more generic. Examples of anchor activities include: independent projects, logic puzzles and games, journaling, creative thinking tasks and activities, and computer programs. Again, it is important to find and create anchor activities that focus on important skills.

As a final note, keep in mind that no amount of training will make differentiation easier if the students do not buy into the idea. For this reason, teachers and students in differentiated classrooms spend a good deal of time discussing the need for differentiation. When students understand why differentiation is necessary and that the classroom can be responsive to them, they are much more likely to take responsibility for making the classroom routines successful.

Effective anchor activities focus on important skills and are not busywork.

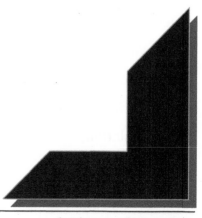

Chapter 4: Language Arts

Tiered Assignments: Exploring a Concept (Loyalty) Through Literature

Overview: These activities demonstrate that students can explore at different levels of complexity and abstractness the concepts or "big ideas" that are highlighted in the novels that they read. This particular set of tasks addresses the concept of *loyalty*, a concept highlighted by novels such as *My Brother Sam is Dead, The Lord of the Flies,* and many others. Students' work with concepts addressed in literature can give teachers ample assessment data regarding students' reading comprehension, their grasp of larger understandings related to both literature and life, and their ability to make connections. Thus, these tasks can be an informative part of the summative evaluation for a novel or literature study.

Standard:
- Connect, compare, and contrast ideas, themes, and issues across texts and with real life

Objectives:
The students will **KNOW**
- The definition of loyalty.
- The relationships among characters in the novel/story.

The students will **UNDERSTAND THAT** (*These statements should be discussed with students prior to their beginning work on the tasks outlined below.*)
- Loyalty is based on experience and values.
- Loyalties can change over time and for different reasons.
- Loyalty can be tested.
- Loyalties can lead to conflict both with others and within oneself.

The students will **BE ABLE TO**
- Explain loyalty and its influences and changes in the story and in real life.
- Discuss the role of loyalty in their own lives.

Basis for Differentiation: Student readiness with regard to:
- students' need for complex and abstract thinking
- the ability to transfer ideas from a novel to the real world

Tier One = lower readiness
Tier Two = middle readiness
Tier Three = higher readiness

Language Arts

Tier One

Choose a statement about loyalty from those we discussed in class, and support it using evidence from the novel. You must cite a variety of situations and events from the novel to support the statement fully. Your supporting evidence must span the entire novel, not just a limited part of it, and you should use quotes as appropriate.

Then prove the same statement is true using evidence from your own life. You must provide details to support the statement, and you should cite as many examples from your life as are appropriate.

Tier Two

Create a continuum, from *not loyal* to *very loyal*, that shows how loyal you think the characters in the novel are to one another and/or to the causes they support.

Now write a statement that explains the criteria that you used to create the continuum, and place the characters' loyalties on it. How did you decide where to put the characters' loyalties on the continuum?

Create a second continuum that shows how loyal you are to the people, groups, and causes in your own life. In writing, explain why you feel more or less loyal in some cases, and describe how you decided where to place your loyalties on your continuum.

Tier Three

Using evidence and details from the novel and from your own life, write a how-to paper titled *How to Determine Your Loyalties and Maintain Them When They Are Tested*. Be sure to address a variety of different loyalties and specific situations that might test them.

Tiered Assignments: Punctuation Marks

Overview: These tasks allow students to demonstrate and further their understanding of particular punctuation marks while working at appropriate levels of challenge and sophistication.

Standards:
- Use a variety of sentence types that are punctuated properly to avoid creating fragments and run-ons

Objectives:
The students will **KNOW**
- The function of a given punctuation mark in a sentence.

The students will **UNDERSTAND THAT**
- A sentence expresses a complete thought containing a subject and verb.
- A sentence can be made more complex with the addition of new clauses.
- Punctuation marks help convey meaning and intent in a piece of writing.
- Punctuation helps to guide the reader in decoding a complex, compound sentence.

The students will **BE ABLE TO**
- Correctly apply punctuation rules to a given sentence.
- Correctly apply punctuation rules to effectively augment a simple sentence with descriptive phrases and clauses (e.g. prepositional phrases, appositives, dependent and independent clauses).

Basis for Differentiation: Student readiness with regard to:
- knowledge of key content
- open-endedness
- abstraction

Note: Actual assignments follow these qualifying remarks.

Tier One = lower readiness

Note to the Teacher: For this level, it is assumed that students need to demonstrate consistent understanding of the basic functions of punctuation. To this end, students at this level will need to practice and master the basics before moving to higher levels of sophisticated thinking about punctuation. The teacher will need, therefore, to provide a straight-forward practice worksheet that targets the skills which match that student's needs, whether it be more work with commas, apostrophes, etc. Practice worksheets are widely and readily available in every grammar instruction book.

Tier Two = middle readiness

Note to the Teacher: Additional punctuation puzzles, such as the ones modeled, can be created by the teacher or students as needed.

Tier Three = higher readiness

Tier One

Before tackling the punctuation review worksheet (*provided by the teacher*), answer the following questions to review your understanding of punctuation's purpose.

1. What key functions do a question mark, exclamation point, semi-colon, and period have in common?
2. List four reasons for using a comma.
3. Apostrophes are NEVER used to make a noun plural. What *are* they used for?
4. What similar purpose do parentheses and dashes share?

- -

Tier Two

Consider the following punctuation puzzles below. For each one, you must carefully consider the punctuation marks to decide what words could logically fit in the blanks to create a complete sentence. Examine the example below as a model.

Example: ____ you ____ , ____ , that ____ house ____ ____ ____ **?**

    Did you know, Sara, that your house is on fire?

1.   ____ ____ **!** ____ ____ has ____ **!**

2. Sandi ____ over ____ ____ 's ____ **.** I ____ ____ gets ____ soon**.**

3. That ____, ____ has three ____ , is ____ ____ **.**

4. I ____ ____ **:** ____ , ____ , and ____ **.**

5. Michael ____ ____ six ____ in ____ ____ **;** ____ is ____ to ____ **!**

Now design and write five punctuation puzzles of your own to share with a partner. (Note: you MUST have an example answer in mind.)

Tier Three

It could be argued that there are several letters in our English alphabet that are not really necessary. Consider the following examples:

- **X is not needed.** The sound made by the letter *x* is equivalent to the sound that can be made by the combination of *c*, *k* and *s*, or *ks*. (Compare: fox *could be* focks.)

- **The QU combination is not needed**. *Q* could be replaced by a *kw* combination. (Compare: queen *could be* kween.)

- **C is not needed**. The sound that the letter *c* makes in certain words could be replaced by an *s*. (Compare: cycle *could be* sycle.) Furthermore, the sound that the letter *c* in makes in most cases could be replaced by a *k*. (Compare: cold *could be* kold.)

Is the same true of punctuation marks? Are there "too many" of these? Consider the list below and find *at least* three that could be eliminated because their essential purpose is already addressed by another type of punctuation. If you are unfamiliar with any of these, look up their meanings/functions.

For each one you eliminate, you must offer a cogent, brief explanation *why* it deserves to be eliminated, and you must offer an example pair of "before and after" sentences that illustrates your idea. Use the models above about letters to guide your own examples.

Eliminate at least three from the following list:

ellipse	**comma**	**semi-colon**	**period**
exclamation point	**apostrophe**	**quotation mark**	**colon**
dash	**hyphen**	**parentheses**	**brackets**
question mark			

Tiered Assignments: Tone and Mood

Overview: These tasks allow students to examine the concept of tone in a written work. Students may work independently or in similar-readiness pairs depending on their preferences. The teacher will need to make available a variety of resources.

Standard:
- Describe the tone and mood (atmosphere) of a given literary work

Objectives:
The students will **KNOW**
- Tone is the attitude a writer takes toward the reader, a subject, or a character.
- Tone and mood (or atmosphere) are closely related, although the latter is the feeling created in the *reader* by the author.
- Diction is the word choice used by an author in a piece of writing.

The students will **UNDERSTAND THAT**
- Tone is conveyed through a writer's choice of words and details (diction).
- A clever author can manipulate a reader's mood with careful selection of the words and details he uses in a piece of writing.
- Some words carry more emotional impact than others, even though their strict literal or dictionary definition may be similar. This distinction is defined as the difference between connotation and denotation.

The students will **BE ABLE TO**
- Concisely describe the tone or mood of a given work.
- Analyze the effects of an author's diction to create a certain tone or mood.

Basis for Differentiation: Student readiness with regard to abstraction

Note to the Teacher: Tone and mood are concepts that many students understand intuitively but often struggle to discuss explicitly. They understand, for example, what a teacher's stern tone of voice means and how they themselves feel (mood) when they are spoken to in such a manner. It is more difficult, however, to describe how a particular tone or mood is created when such words are conveyed only on paper. Students need the opportunity to see how word choice can cause a reaction, and they need further opportunities to develop a vocabulary that can be used to describe both tone and mood. To this end, the following focus activity is an especially effective way to introduce these concepts to the whole class before the following tiered lessons are implemented.

Record a series of TV advertisements. (Note: Although any sort of ad will work, those that promote prescription medications are especially effective for this activity. There are numerous such ads on during most primetime shows. Similarly, during election campaigns, political ads would be an effective tool.) Play a few of the ads in class and have students analyze them to answer the following questions. The fruits of this discussion get at the meat of what defines tone and mood.
- *What is this ad trying to get you to do? Buy something? Do something?*
- *Who is the product intended for? What words or phrases are used to help sell this ad to that specific population?*
- *What images are used in these ads? How do these images help promote a positive (or negative) feeling about the product?*
- *Does this ad attempt to get you to do something using a promise of benefits? Or does it play on fears of the viewer?*

Tier One

Find at least five pictures that, in your opinion, convey a definite mood/atmosphere or, alternatively, express a particular tone of the artist. You may choose from magazine ads, historical photos, etc., or your teacher may provide you with pictures.

For each picture, state in a single word what you feel represents the mood/tone of the picture. Then list any details you observed in the picture that help to create that mood/tone.

Tier Two

Using the selections given to you by the teacher*, identify in a single word the tone and then mood of the passages. For each selection, supply quotes and words from the text that support your claims. For example, you might claim that an image of a man stranded in a desert creates a tone of desperation.

* Some authors are known for their ability to effectively create a mood. Stephen King, for example, excels at the horror genre, while Dave Barry is known for his humor. You might also investigate first-hand accounts as supplied by newspaper stories or historical documents such as *The Diary of Anne Frank*.

Tier Three

For an author to create a specific tone or mood, he must choose his words carefully. Unfortunately not all words have the same emotional impact on a reader even though their strict dictionary meanings might be essentially the same. For example, *aversion* and *disgust* have similar literal meanings. However, *aversion* evokes feelings of only a mild unpleasantness while *disgust* carries a harder, more intense feeling of revulsion. This difference in literal meaning versus emotional meaning is expressed by the distinction of a word's denotation versus its connotation.

Consider the words below, all of which have a similar denotation. For each set, describe how the emotional tones of the words differ, as demonstrated in the example above. You might find a thesaurus helpful for this activity.

cuisine *vs.* meal	obstinate *vs.* pigheaded	hard-nosed *vs.* strict
imperfect *vs.* defective	young *vs.* immature	burdensome *vs.* weight
collect *vs.* hoard	hybrid *vs.* mongrel	resign *vs.* surrender

RAFT: Characterization in A Wrinkle in Time

Overview: These RAFT assignments ask students to describe and analyze the characteristics and behavior of characters in A Wrinkle in Time by Madeline L'Engle. Each assignment requires students to apply and synthesize what they know about a character or several characters from their reading of the novel and from class activities and discussions. This RAFT could be used in conjunction with a more formal assessment at the end of the study of this novel. Because the assignments are based on student learning profile differences, allow students to choose which assignments they will complete.

Standards:
- Respond to fiction, nonfiction, poetry, and drama using interpretive, critical, and evaluative processes
- Interact with the text before, during, and after reading
- Identify and analyze characteristics and elements of fiction

Objectives:
The students will **KNOW**
- Literary elements used in fiction.
- Characters in A Wrinkle in Time.

The students will **UNDERSTAND THAT**
- Fictional characters have distinct personalities.
- We can describe and make inferences about characters' personalities and behaviors based on their words and actions.
- Authors create characters and manipulate their actions to further the plot.

The students will **BE ABLE TO**
- Describe characters.
- Analyze characters' words and actions.
- Make inferences.
- Justify thinking and defend choices.
- Think creatively.
- Work independently.

Basis for Differentiation: Student learning profile (Gardner's Multiple Intelligences):
#1 – Visual/Spatial, Verbal
#2 – Interpersonal, Mathematical/Logical
#3 – Intrapersonal, Verbal
#4 – Musical, Interpersonal

Characterization in _A Wrinkle in Time_

ROLE	AUDIENCE	FORMAT	TOPIC
Police profiler	The public	Wanted poster with "photo" and detailed description	Reward! Who this character is, why he/she is wanted, and how to track him/her down
Dinner party host/hostess	Dinner party guests (8-10 characters from _A Wrinkle in Time_)	Seating chart	Where you're all sitting and why
A character from <u>A Wrinkle in Time</u>	Madeline L'Engle	Letter	What I like and don't like about the things you made me do and say
Soundtrack creator	Record company executive	Song list (including at least 10 songs with explanations about each)	If this character's life were a movie, here's the sound-track...and WHY

RAFT: Literary Theme

Overview: These RAFT options give students an opportunity to apply their knowledge of theme and to practice determining the overarching theme of a piece of literature. The tasks can be used with any piece of literature containing a strong theme. To effectively assess students' understanding of theme, require students to complete their chosen tasks individually, rather than with partners or in small groups.

Standards:
- Read and analyze a variety of literature to identify format, text structure, and main idea
- Use literary terms in describing and analyzing selections

Objectives:
The students will **KNOW**
- Theme is the central message or lesson of a written selection.
- A piece of literature might discuss a variety of topics and might, therefore, have a number of themes.

The students will **UNDERSTAND THAT**
- A theme is best expressed in a sentence or two, while a topic is a single word.

The students will **BE ABLE TO**
- Accurately identify and describe a passage's theme, as well as the topics that passage discusses.
- Defend an identified choice of theme(s) with rationale from the text.

Basis for Differentiation: Student learning profile with specific regard to interest in the tasks described below.

📄 Introduction to the Options – Literary Theme

Theme is the central idea or insight of a work of literature. It is important to understand that a theme is not the same as a topic or subject of a work. In fact, theme is always expressed as one or two sentences, whereas a topic is just a single word. For example, the *topic* of a book might be love or honesty, but that same book's *theme* is likely to be a stronger message the author is conveying about those topics. For example, an author's message about love might be: *Love can endure any obstacle.*

Many works have more than one theme. Although, occasionally some stories or poems might have a clearly stated theme, most works do not. It is up to you, the reader, to decide this for yourself.

Literary Theme

ROLE	AUDIENCE	FORMAT	TOPIC
Manufacturer	Car drivers	Bumper sticker	The theme of my book is…
Newspaper editor	Newspaper readers	Newspaper headline	New best-selling book's message is…
Author	Himself	Post-It™ Note	Reminder: What my book's central lesson is supposed to be…
Publishing editor	Author of book	Email comment text box (no more than 120 words)	I think we need to clarify. The point of your story is…?
Jeopardy question writer	Jeopardy contestant	Answer to a question	The theme of the book is best stated as…
Letter writer	Correspondent	P.S. of a letter	I just read a great book. Its theme is…
Book reviewer	Potential buyer of the book	Back cover blurb	The central lesson of this book is…
Online book seller	Potential buyer	Online customer review	Five stars! I loved this book! Its theme is…

Think-Tac-Toe: Cause and Effect

Overview: These interactive projects provide students with the opportunity to consider their own understanding of cause and effect. Many students unfortunately confuse a plot's *order of events* with *cause and effect*. The two are not the same, however, and mis-identifying these can cause students trouble as they move on to more sophisticated analyses of literary works, including analyzing character motivation, discussing a book's plot structure, making skillful predictions, and pinpointing the sources of conflict. Students may work in small cooperative learning groups to develop and carry out the projects, or they may work to complete them independently. This is for the teacher to decide. Allowing students to choose the groupings, small group or independent, would add an additional element of learning profile differentiation to these tasks.

Standards: The student will:
- Use a text's structure or progression of ideas to identify such relationships as cause and effect
- Determine a text's main (or major ideas) and identify how those ideas are supported, either strongly or weakly, with details

Objectives:
The students will **KNOW**
- Key terms associated with a discussion of cause and effect, including the following: cause, effect, fallacy.

The students will **UNDERSTAND THAT**
- There is a significant difference between a simple description of a story or a tale's order of events and the more complex cause and effect relationships that may exist in that same selection.
- Authors sometimes manipulate a reader to falsely establish a cause and effect relationship.
- Key words and phrases (such as "so," "because," "If... then") are markers for identifying cause and effect relationships.

The students will **BE ABLE TO**
- Demonstrate effective communication skills that reflect an understanding of cause and effect relationships.
- Paraphrase and summarize text to recall, inform, or organize ideas.
- Make inferences and support them with text evidence and experience.
- Read and represent text information in different ways, including using such devices as graphic organizers.

Basis for Differentiation: Student learning profile (Gardner's Multiple Intelligences)

📄 Introduction to the Tasks – Cause and Effect

These activities will help you analyze the causes and effects of a situation, an event, or a trend.

Most of us think about cause and effect in a number of ways on a daily basis – when we try to figure out why a parent is so upset or when we consider the consequences of missing a scheduled sports' team practice.

The ability to correctly analyze cause and effect helps a doctor consider how a particular course of treatment may benefit a patient. It helps a business CEO figure out why a company's profits might be slumping. It helps a manager figure out how to motivate his employees effectively.

Cause and effect combine critical and creative thinking skills.

Cause and Effect

Logical – Mathematical	Naturalist	Verbal - Linguistic
Cause and effect relationships are seldom neat and clean. Many times, a single effect is the result of a number of causes. For example, if a man orders hot coffee at a drive-through and then also hits a pothole in the road, THEN he might get burned. It takes the combination of both of these events to lead to the man's injury. Graphically, this might look like the following: Event A + Event B → Event C Create a written explanation that could be represented by the cause and effect chains listed below. 1. A → B + C 2. A + B → C + D 3. A + B + C → D +E 4. A → B → C + D 5. A + B → C → D + E	There are many examples of cause and effect in the natural world. If a plant is not given enough water or sunlight, it will die. Think about natural systems you've studied in science classes. Describe at least 5 examples of cause and effect, as demonstrated in the example above. If you get stuck, you might consider cycles in the following areas: ■ Weather ■ Photosynthesis ■ Geology ■ The Human Body	Advertisers make their living by promoting cause and effect relationships, some of which are accurate and some of which may not be 100% truthful. Some advertisers build their ideas on fallacies. (A *fallacy* is a cause and effect relationship that is not accurate. For example, if a baseball player eats a red M&M right before going up to bat and then hits a homerun, he might then superstitiously assume that eating the candy before batting was responsible for the run.) Find examples of advertisements where a cause and effect relationship is either stated or implied. Identify the claims being made, and then decide whether they are legitimate or not. Consider product advertisements and, if available, political ads as well.
Visual – Spatial The saying goes that "A picture is worth a thousand words." It is true that a clever artist can capture, in a visual format, ideas that would take pages to describe in writing. Find five works of art whose images express a cause and effect relationship. Identify these clearly, using references to the picture. You may use photographs or original productions.	**Have your own idea?** **See your teacher to explain it and get it approved.**	**Bodily - Kinesthetic** Sometimes a player makes a play that is so great it changes the outcome of a game that was otherwise considered unwinable. Research 5 examples of Great Plays in Sports History. Briefly describe the scenario and then clearly identify the cause and effect relationship to explain how this play affected the outcome of the event, either for good or bad.
Musical - Rhythmic Find five pieces of music whose lyrics express a cause and effect relationship. Identify these clearly, using quotes from the song. *Example:* In the Beatles' song "Imagine," John Lennon proposes the idea that, if there were "no possession," then there would be "no greed or hunger" among men.	**Intrapersonal** Consider yourself in your surroundings and then brainstorm a list of *causes* for the following: ■ Conflict in schools today ■ Teens choosing a particular fashion ■ Why one of your school's sports teams is performing well/poorly ■ Why kids and parents disagree ■ Why teens have to wait until they are 16 to get a driver's license	**Interpersonal** You are a part of the world in which you live. Your actions have an effect on a number of others in unique ways. Brainstorm a list of *effects* for the following: ■ Not having a dress code in schools ■ Stopping illegal immigration ■ Closing a shopping mall ■ Giving free access to the internet to everyone in the country ■ Eliminating PE from the school day

Tiered Think-Tac-Toes: Novel Study

Overview: These tiered Think-Tac-Toes can be used with a wide range of novels. For each tier, the rows focus on different literary elements (these are the same for all three tiers): characterization, setting, and plot. Students are assigned a particular tier and then choose one task from each row on their Think-Tac-Toe to complete a total of three tasks. While they can work on their tasks in any order they choose, each student will ultimately be working with all three literary elements included on the Think-Tac-Toes. While this approach provides students with quite a bit of choice based on their learning profiles, it also allows teachers to challenge students appropriately based on their readiness levels.

Standards:
- Respond to fiction, nonfiction, poetry, and drama using interpretive, critical, and evaluative processes
- Interact with the text before, during, and after reading
- Identify and analyze characteristics and elements of fiction

Objectives:
The students will **KNOW**
- Literary elements (characterization, setting, plot) of a particular story.

The students will **UNDERSTAND THAT**
- Fictional characters have distinct personalities.
- We can describe and make inferences about characters' personalities and behaviors based on their words and actions.
- The setting of a story plays an important role in the events that take place in the story.
- Stories often have themes and lessons that relate to the real world.

The students will **BE ABLE TO**
- Make personal connections to a story.
- Describe characters, settings, and plots.
- Analyze characters' words and actions.
- Make inferences.
- Justify thinking and defend choices.
- Compare and contrast.
- Work independently.
- Use planning strategies to complete projects.

Basis for Differentiation: Student readiness (Bloom's Taxonomy and the *Equalizer*) and student learning profile (Gardner's Multiple Intelligences)

Tier One = lower readiness
Tier Two = middle readiness
Tier Three = higher readiness

Tier 1   Novel Study   Think-Tac-Toe

Rank order the characters in the story from your most favorite to your least favorite. Which character do you like the most? Why? Which character do you like the least? Why?	Create a cartoon strip using some of the characters. What will the characters say to one another? What will they do? Be sure that the characters maintain the personalities and behaviors that they demonstrate in the story.	Interview one of the important characters from the story. What questions will you ask him or her? How will the character answer your questions? Be sure to include both your questions and the character's answers.
What would you do if your family needed to move to a place in the story? How would you feel about the move? Write a paragraph to describe what you would say and do if this happened.	Create a collage that fully describes the setting of the story using at least 12 pictures from magazines and newspapers. Label the pictures so that viewers understand the story's setting and why you chose the pictures you did.	Design a flag for a place of your choosing in the story. Make sure that your flag "tells" something important about the place. Use pictures and words to describe this place as completely as you can.
Summarize the story fully in 50 words or fewer. Be sure to tell the "highlights" as you see them. If you had only very limited space, what would be most important to tell about this story?	Create a crossword puzzle based on the events in the story. Be sure that your clues include accurate information. Allow a classmate to try to complete your puzzle.	Create a wordless picture book that illustrates the important events in the story. How can you retell this story using only illustrations? Create an original cover for your book, too.

Tier 2   Novel Study   Think-Tac-Toe

Create an original dialogue between two of the story's characters as they work to solve a problem. Make sure that both characters speak and act as they do in the story. What problem are they trying to solve? What will they say to each other? How will each of them try to solve the problem?	What would you do if one or more of the characters moved next door to you? How would this change your neighborhood? What would you do? What would you say to the character(s)? Would you be friends? Why or why not?	Retell an important event in the story from one character's point of view. Which event and character will you choose and why? How will the character report this event? What will he or she say about it? What will he or she have to tell us about other characters in the story?
Compare the story's main setting to one of the following places: a) your school, b) your town, c) or your neighborhood. How are these places alike and different? Provide many details to support your thinking.	Do you think that the story could have taken place somewhere else? Why or why not? If so, what are some other possible settings for the story and why would they be possible? If not, explain in detail why the story's setting must not be changed.	Create a print advertisement for a magazine that "sells" a place in the story. This ad should make people want to move there. How will you make a place in the story seem like a great place to live? Your ad should describe this place completely and accurately.
Do you think there is a lesson to be learned from events in this story? What is the lesson and who do you think would benefit from reading this story in order to learn this lesson? What other stories also teach this lesson?	Find and cut out newspaper and magazine headlines that can be used to describe the events in this story. Use them to create a collage or a scrapbook. Write a detailed statement next to each headline explaining why you chose it.	What are the two most important events in the story? What makes these events so important? What happens because of them? How would the story be different without them?

Tier 3   Novel Study   Think-Tac-Toe

Create a monologue about the world that the main character might deliver. What would he or she want to say about the world today? What issues would he or she choose to focus on and why? Be sure to act and speak as the main character does.	If you could change the actions of one character in the story, which character would it be and why? What would you change about the character's actions and how would you do it? How would you want him or her to behave?	Imagine that you are an advice columnist like Dear Abby. What questions would the characters have for you? How would you respond to them? Be sure to focus on the kinds of problems the characters face in the story or might face in real life.
Different places can evoke different moods and feelings. Come up with a creative way to explain how the mood of this story is affected by the setting and by changes in the setting. Use vibrant adjectives to help us understand the relationship between setting and mood in this story.	Imagine the story takes place in a different time period. For example, what would the story be like if it took place 100 years earlier? How about 100 years in the future? Be creative, but don't change anything but the time period.	Imagine that you are a tour guide leading visitors on a walking tour around the setting of this story. Create your script highlighting important places and events in the story. Where will you take the visitors and why? What will you tell them?
Imagine that you are a news reporter on the 6 o'clock news. You've been assigned to report on an event in the story. Your account must be interest-ing, accurate, and entertaining. What will you say? What visuals will you use to add flair and information to your report?	Write newspaper accounts of a major event in the story that would appeal to each of the following people: a) a young child, b) a 100-year-old grandmother, and c) a person lost on a deserted island. Your account must be informative and entertaining to your readers.	How does the title of the story relate to the events in the story? Why do you think the author chose it? Do you think this is the best title for the story? Come up with two alternate titles for the story and explain in detail why they are good choices.

Complex Instruction: Conflict

Overview: These Complex Instruction tasks enable students to work in mixed-ability, learning profile-based groups of three or four in order to carry out a number of tasks that encourage greater understanding of conflict through the exploration of it in the real world. The tasks focus on the creation of products that illustrate the group's understanding of both internal and external conflict. As a complex instruction activity, students are required to work both cooperatively and independently to complete the various assignments below.

Standard:
- Analyze how an author utilizes conflict in a literary work to build character motivation and create dramatic tension in a story

Objectives:
The students will **KNOW**
- Conflict can be described as either external or internal.
- Most stories contain both internal and external conflict.

The students will **UNDERSTAND THAT**
- Conflict is an essential element to any story, and the results of conflict are what ultimately lead to a story's climax.
- Internal conflict is reflected by the worries or fears that a character expresses.
- External conflict can be grouped in at least three different ways: (1) as a struggle between one character and another in the story; (2) as a struggle between a character and a larger element of society, and (3) as a struggle between a character and some element in nature.

The students will **BE ABLE TO**
- Create written material to effectively convey a deep understanding of both *types* of conflict as well as different *sources* of conflict.
- Form opinions from observations that have been made as a result of close reading and analysis of character motivation.
- Work cooperatively and independently.

Basis for Differentiation: Student learning profile (Gardner's Multiple Intelligences and student personality types)

📄 Introduction to All Tasks

Conflict is the struggle or clash between opposing characters, forces, or emotions. In external conflict, a character struggles against some outside force. This may be another character, society in general, or a problem in nature. An internal conflict, on the other hand, is a struggle among the needs, desires, or emotions within a single character. Through the activities, your group members will explore these understandings about conflict.

Internal Conflict: Man vs. Himself, or "Don't Be A Worry Wart!" (Intrapersonal)

Create a poster that has on it the likeness of person that the whole class is likely to know. It may be one of the members of your group (if you are comfortable with this) or it may be a poster that represents someone famous, perhaps a Hollywood celebrity. Around this person, list at least ten (10) worries, fears, etc. that you feel represent this individual's internal conflicts. For example: a Hollywood celebrity might worry about the success or failure of his next big movie release the night before its premier.

External Conflict: Man vs. Man, or "Dear Abby" (Interpersonal, Verbal-linguistic)

Imagine a situation in which a person at work has a conflict with another co-worker. Brainstorm a list of potential conflicts two office workers might have. You are encouraged to be imaginative but not outlandish. Now write a "Dear Abby" letter describing, with *rich detail*, the exact nature of the conflict. Then write the response that Ms. Abby might supply to address the concerns of this letter's author. This response should include a solution, or solutions, as appropriate.

External Conflict: Man vs. Nature, or "Get Me Out of Here!" (Naturalist, Logical-mathematical)

There are many stories of people who, trapped in a variety of bizarre circumstances, have found themselves fighting for their own survival against harsh conditions of Mother Nature. Conduct research to find at least three (3) of these survival stories on which you will become an expert. Then summarize, in paragraph format, the unique stories you have investigated. For each one, include a list of "survival items" that helped the individuals survive their life-and-death challenges.

External Conflict: Man vs. Society, or "What's All the Fuss?" (Visual-spatial)

Societies are built upon the actions and reactions of the people who compose that group. Indeed, history is full of people who have become famous for standing up for an idea that they saw as *essential*-- perhaps even before the rest of society recognized it. Martin Luther King, for example, stood up for equal rights and equal treatment of the African-American population in our country. Your task is to research other examples of famous figures (American or otherwise) who, through their own sense of right and wrong, stood up against society. Use the fruits of your research to create a collage that graphically presents your research on these people, complete with images that show these individuals' conflicts, desires, achievements, etc. On the back of the poster, annotate your collage's images with sentences that explain who your figures are and the exact nature of their conflict with society.

Complex Instruction: Direct and Indirect Characterization

Overview: These Complex Instruction tasks enable students to work in mixed-ability, learning profile-based groups in order to carry out a number of tasks that get at the key differences between direct and indirect characterization. The essential element of this assignment focuses on the collaborative creation of a report/presentation on a famous individual to be presented to the rest of the class. The overall task requires research which group members can do together. After this initial research is completed, students work on the duties listed below according to their own choosing. In this way, students are required to work both cooperatively and independently as they create different types of products.

Standard:
- Analyze how an author builds characters in a literary work (including their traits, motivations, conflicts, and points of view) through direct and indirect characterization

Objectives:
The students will **KNOW**
- A character is an individual in a story, poem, or play.
- The differences between direct and indirect characterization.

The students will **UNDERSTAND THAT**
- A writer can reveal a character's personality by simply telling the reader what the character is like (bold, weak, etc.). This is called *direct* characterization.
- A writer can reveal what a character is like by *indirect* means, including:
  - Describing how the character looks and dresses
  - Letting the reader hear the character speak
  - Letting the reader listen to the character's inner thoughts and feelings
  - Revealing what other characters have to say or think about the character
- Indirect characterization requires the reader to put clues together to figure out what a character is like.
- Compiled information and knowledge can be used to raise additional and as-yet-unanswered questions.

The students will **BE ABLE TO**
- Conduct research.
- Create written material to effectively convey information of a specific type to an audience.
- Form and revise questions for investigations, including questions arising from readings, assignments, and other cross-curricular units of study.
- Use multiple sources, including electronic texts, experts, and print resources, to locate information relevant to research questions.
- Produce research projects and reports in effective formats for various audiences.
- Work cooperatively and independently.

Basis for Differentiation: Student learning profile (Gardner's Multiple Intelligences and student personality types)

Note to the Teacher: These activities explore the ways in which authors convey the broad concept of "character" to a reader.

With this in mind, the teacher should note that the first four tasks engage students in activities that require them to convey information to an audience through *indirect* means (as outlined in the objectives stated above).

The last task, the written report, illustrates the concept of *direct characterization*. With this in mind, these activities could be conducted as an illustrative introductory activity, *before* distinguishing the difference between direct and indirect characterization. In this way, the fruits of the students' work could later be used as "talking points" for the instructor as he/she teaches the lesson(s) about characterization methods.

📄 Introduction to All Tasks – Direct and Indirect Characterization

You and your group members will become the experts on a famous person, living or dead. You may either choose this individual (with teacher approval) or select one from the list supplied by the teacher.

You must keep your group's selection secret! Together, you and your group members will work to complete the tasks described. Each piece will be shared with the rest of the class, whose job it will be to guess your famous person.

Be sure to provide hints about whom you are describing, but do not be too obvious. The more you know about your person, the more hints you can give and the more clever you will be able to make your presentation.

Do *not* skimp on the information-gathering portion of this task in an effort to hurry to the tasks described. Finally, read and carefully consider the tasks *before* you select your famous person. Knowing first what you will have to do with the information you gather might help you make a better selection.

Task One: Let's Talk
(the Conversationalists in the group)

Create a 2-minute conversation between two individuals. In this scene, the two people must talk about the famous person without naming who it is. This conversation might tell the class about the mystery person's habits, background experiences, personality, etc. Be clever with your selection of who is talking in this scene. Are they friends of the individual? Colleagues? Fans? Mother and father? Furthermore, place this conversation in some sort of context. Did these two people just get back from a visit with the mystery person? Did they just see him/her at an event? Did one just get a letter from him/her?

Task Two: The Monolgue – the "Pitch"
(the Ham in the group)

Your task is to write and deliver a 1-minute speech in which you assume the role of the mystery person. In this monologue, you should share aloud the inner thoughts, feelings or reactions you may have about any issues or events that are especially important to you in your role as the mystery person. Also be sure to include any particular accent or physical mannerisms that may be an aspect of your individual. Your goal is to let the class know more about yourself by letting them see how your mind works.

Task Three: Time for My Close-up
(the Artist in the group)

Your task is to create a poster (or some other teacher-approved visual) that provides the class with visual clues/information about your group's mystery person. The informational power of this task rests in the details! Be sure to consider style of dress/uniform, poses, appropriate background selection, as well as props that individual may hold or use. The class may ask questions about your visual to help gain more information.

Task Four: Actions Speak Louder than Words
(the "I Just Can't Stay Still!" person in the group)

Your task is to create a series of hints about who the character could be by focusing on the *activities* that your mystery person might carry out on a typical day. You may not speak during your presentation. You may only mime actions that hint at what sort of occupation your person is known for. Thus, if he/she is known for work in the sciences, you might demonstrate a person tinkering with test tubes and solutions in a laboratory.

Task Five: Reporting, Sir!
(the Wallflower in the group)

Your task is to condense all of your group's research efforts into a single-page biographical paper, similar to any standard encyclopedia entry. As you write about your mystery person and his/her accomplishments, be certain that you draw a blank line wherever the person's name would appear. This piece will be shared with the class last and should be the one piece of your group's project that summarizes the greatest amount of information about your individual in one place. It should cap off your group's efforts and thus contain the largest number of straight-forward hints about who your group's mysterious person is. This will not be orally presented. Instead, you will give a copy of this report to your teacher who will make enough copies for the rest of the class to read and keep for notes.

Complex Instruction: Create-an-Infomercial

Overview: These Complex Instruction tasks enable students to work in mixed-ability, learning profile-based groups of four in order to practice and demonstrate a number of research and presentation skills. The essential element of this problem rests in designing an effective promotional campaign to help sell either an existing or brand-new, student-designed product. Students will work collaboratively to create a final product. Each task requires some research, which group members can do together. As this research is completed, students work on tasks of their choosing. In this way, students are required to work both cooperatively and independently as they answer different types of questions and complete different types of products.

Standards:
- Explore informational materials that are read, heard, and/or viewed by studying the characteristics of informational works and restating and summarizing information
- Make inferences and/or draw conclusions
- Generate questions
- Prepare individual and/or group essays and presentations that use evaluative technique
- Prepare individual and/or group essays and presentations that focus on the diagnosis of a problem and possible solutions

Objectives:
The students will **KNOW**
- Vocabulary: marketing, promotion, goods, services, "pitch," target audience.

The students will **UNDERSTAND THAT**
- Marketing is the process of planning and executing the conception, pricing, promotion, and distribution of ideas, goods, services, organizations, and events to create and maintain relationships that will satisfy individual and organizational objectives.
- Information helpful in effective marketing can be attained and conveyed through a variety of resources, including books, Internet, electronic databases, and CD-ROMs.
- A "pitch" is an essential tool in marketing, whose purpose is to effectively and concisely convey information in a manner designed to sway an individual to adopt a particular opinion.
- Having a firm control of the facts, audience awareness, clear ideas, and relevant and coherent reasons are rhetorical factors that effectively sway audiences.
- Effective marketing of a product depends upon carefully matching a product to a consumer market.
- Effective marketing of a product depends upon describing a product in a way that demonstrates uniqueness in the market.
- Comparing and/or contrasting is an essential way of determining the importance and accuracy of information in a given reading selection or presentation.

The students will **BE ABLE TO**
- Conduct research.
- Create written material to effectively convey information to a specific type of audience.
- Compare and contrast the effectiveness of various presentations.
- Analyze data taken from a survey.
- Synthesize information to solve a problem.
- Work cooperatively and independently.

Basis for Differentiation: Student learning profile (Gardner's Multiple Intelligences as well as the need to think divergently) with some flexibility to address readiness differences (for instance, the need for structure versus open-endedness and clearly-defined problems versus less-defined ones)

Note to the Teacher: This project's core concepts are based on the classic late-night television infomercial. Some students will be familiar with this unique type of advertising, while others will not. As students engage in the various steps of these cooperative learning activities, it will be helpful for the teacher to provide visual examples of such advertisements for those who are less familiar. Therefore, as a priming activity, before this project is handed to the students, the teacher might wish to record and show a segment of the Home Shopping Network or QVC. Similarly, great sample products with advertising "blurbs" can be found in mailing catalogues and on numerous internet sites like www.asseenontv.com .

Furthermore, to simulate the function of a company's CEO and Board of Directors, it is intended that each group will present its efforts to the class after Task Two and then again after Task Three. The teacher may, of course, alter this to suit his/her own objectives or time constraints.

🖹 Introduction to All Tasks – Create an Infomercial

You and your group members are employees of JGL Corporation, a company that delivers unique and creative products to a general market. Your products cover a wide range of needs, from beauty supplies and exercise needs to automotive care and home accessories.

Recent reports from the CEO of the company indicate that overall profits for JGL Corporation have slumped for the third quarter in a row. Your help is needed! As the product design and analysis team of JGL Corp., your job is to help revive the company's sagging performance by bringing to market a product that will significantly boost sales.

The tasks will help your group make decisions about how to help JGL Corporation regain its footing. The results of your efforts here will culminate in a group presentation about your selected product (Tasks Two and Three). It will be delivered to the CEO of JGL Corporation (your teacher) and the company's Board of Directors (your classmates).

Task One: Product Research
(logical-mathematical, verbal-linguistic)

Before you can find that "perfect product" to restore JGL's profits, you will need to know what kinds of products already exist in the market. It is tempting at this stage to just jump right in and create a brand-new idea. Be careful! A thorough review of what is already out there can save you a lot of trouble later. There are already thousands of unique products for sale. Which areas of the market are already well targeted? Health care? Sports and hobby equipment? Technology accessories? Which products sell the best?

Your job is to research the infomercial product market and then prepare a written report for your CEO's review. This report should be limited to a single page of writing (the CEO does not have time to read more than this, so keep it concise!). This report must contain answers to the following questions.

- What are the general categories of product marketing? (Example: "Kitchen gadgets" might be one. What are others?)
- What are a few sample products in each category?
- What is the price range of these sample products?
- Who are these selected products generally marketed to? (Example: Do-It-Yourselfers? Retirees? College students?)
- If possible, can you determine which types of products seem to sell the best?
- Do there seem to be any "holes" in the market – an area where you find relatively few products available? If so, identify them for your CEO.

- -

Task Two: Product Selection – the "Pitch"
(visual-spatial, interpersonal)

Your task is to select one product that you feel is strong enough to help boost the sales at JGL. Using the results of the research stage in the first task, you will need to consider the following as you make this very important decision: Do you really need to invent something completely brand new, or could you select an older product and remarket it with a fresh twist? Regardless of your choice, you'll need to convince your boss and the Board of Directors. To do this, your group must "pitch" its idea.

Create a summary PowerPoint presentation. The PowerPoint should be four slides in length and should convey the following information about your selected product:

- Slide 1: What is the name of the product? In a single sentence, what does the product do? How much does the product cost?
- Slide 2: Who will buy this product?
- Slide 3: What other products out there might compete with yours?
- Slide 4: List FIVE reasons why your group believes this product is an especially good choice for your targeted consumers.

Task Three: Sample Ads
(visual-spatial, musical-rhythmic, verbal-linguistic, interpersonal)

Once the CEO has approved your product choice, you will need to consider how it could be made appealing to the consumer. Your company is particularly interested in marketing this product through the JGL mailing catalogue and by placing advertisements on radio. Your job is to create the text for these ads.

- Using the sample catalogues provided in class, create a product description that would draw a consumer to your item.
- Write the text for a sixty-second radio spot. Make sure it conveys the product name, function, and cost. The work you did in Task Two might be helpful. Furthermore, the commercial should start and finish with a short jingle about the product. The commercial can last no longer than sixty seconds and must be understandable (so don't read too fast!).

- -

Task Four: Survey Team
(intrapersonal, interpersonal, logical mathematical)

You are almost done! The pitch has been made, the ads are in place! It is time to see how effective your ideas have been. To do this, you will need to create and conduct a survey.

Are there tasks (above) that you think your group did an especially good job on? Are there places in this process that you had concerns about? Create a survey and see what others in your class think! Your survey should be limited to ten essential "Yes-No" questions that will help you gather information about the following broad ideas:

- The effectiveness of the ads (both the catalogue and the radio spot)
- The usefulness of the product you chose
- How effective this product will be in raising the profits JGL

Once you have administered this survey to your classmates, compile the results and present your findings to the CEO. Your report must include:

- A list of all the questions you asked
- How many "yeses" and "nos" there were for each question
- A one-paragraph analysis/self-reflection on how this project went for your team. In this paragraph reflect on the results of the survey and offer your own reflections.

Chapter 5: Math

Tiered Assignment: Graphing and Data Analysis

Overview: These tiered activities ask students to apply their skill with graphing and data collection. The readiness level for the activities is modified based on the complexity of the types of graphs selected at each level. It is assumed that these assignments will be offered after instruction on reading and constructing graphs is completed. Students may work independently or in similar-readiness, cooperative learning groups to complete the tasks, with the teacher making that determination.

Standards:
- Collect, organize, analyze, and display data in graphic format
- Select, create and use appropriate graphical representations of data

Objectives:
The students will **KNOW**
- The value of representing mathematical data in a visual format.
- A variety of graphic methods exists to organize and display data.

The students will **UNDERSTAND THAT**
- Interpreting graphs allows one to analyze quantities of data with minimal time expended.
- Collecting and organizing data to construct a graph develops valuable research skills.
- Graphs reduce a large amount of data into a small, manageable space.
- Graphs are easily adaptable to a variety of technological formats.

The students will **BE ABLE TO**
- Collect data and construct a graph that accurately displays the data.
- Analyze and interpret a graph to determine the information it conveys.
- Distinguish between a bar, line, and circle graph and determine which is best suited for the data collected.

Basis for Differentiation: Student readiness with regard to:
- understanding of various graphic formats
- higher-level thinking skills
- open-endedness
- sophistication of data collection

Tier One = lower readiness
Tier Two = middle readiness
Tier Three = higher readiness

Math

Tier One

Choose one of the following sources to gather a set of data:
- The website of a favorite sports team. The data may be generated by the team, such as win-loss records over a period of years, or by individual players.
- The Weather Channel website. There is a wealth of weather data listed here for individual cities that can be found as you explore this site. The highs or lows of different cities can be compared, or you can collect data for one specific city.
- The United States Census Bureau's website (www.census.gov) contains a large variety of data on people who live in the United States. Explore this website to find a topic of interest to you.
- The Bureau of Transportation website on airline statistics (www.bts.gov/programs/airline_information/)
- The World Almanac for Kids (www.worldalmanacforkids.com/explore/index.html)

After you have chosen a set of data, use it to create a bar or line graph. You may generate this graph using a computer program or design it on 5-inch graph paper. Give the graph a title and label both the horizontal axis and vertical axis. Once the graph is constructed, compose five interesting questions that your graph answers. Trade your graph and questions with another student so that you each can interpret each other's graphs.

Tier Two

Choose one of the following sources to gather a set of data that is based on percentages:
- The website of a favorite sports team. The data may be generated by the team, such as win-loss records over a period of years, or by individual players.
- The Weather Channel website. There is a wealth of weather data listed here for individual cities that can be found as you explore this site. The highs or lows of different cities can be compared, or you can collect data for one specific city.
- The United States Census Bureau's website (www.census.gov) contains a large variety of data on people who live in the United States. Explore this website to find a topic of interest to you.
- The Bureau of Transportation website on airline statistics (www.bts.gov/programs/airline_information/)
- The World Almanac for Kids (www.worldalmanacforkids.com/explore/index.html)

After you have chosen a set of data, use it to create a circle graph. Give the graph a title and label the different sections of the circle. Once the graph is constructed, compose five interesting questions that your graph answers. Trade your graph and questions with another student so that you each can interpret each other's graphs.

Tier Three

Choose a topic from the list below and conduct a survey of students in your school. Collect data from at least 25 students. Topics you may choose to survey include:

- What type of pets do you have in your home?
- Which ice cream flavor would be your first choice when ordering at an ice cream store? (Give students a choice from 10 popular flavors – vanilla, chocolate, butter pecan, strawberry, chocolate chip, cookies and cream, vanilla fudge ripple, pralines and cream, mint chocolate chip, rocky road.)
- Which toppings would you choose if you were ordering a pizza? You may choose as many as you would order on one pizza. (Give students a choice from 10 popular toppings – cheese, pepperoni, chicken, sausage, ham, ground beef, mushrooms, green pepper, pineapple, onions.)
- What kind of music do you listen to most often? (Give students the choice of classic rock and roll, rap, hip hop, top forty, country, alternative rock, classical, or *"I don't listen to music."*)

You may choose another topic of your own choice with the approval of your teacher.

Once you have chosen your topic, design a way to organize your data. When it is collected, determine the fractional part of the whole sample that each response represents. Turn these fractions into percentages, using a calculator if desired.

Construct a circle graph to display the results of your survey.

Compose two paragraphs, one describing your experience conducting the survey and the other analyzing the results. Include in the second paragraph what conclusions can be drawn from the data concerning the students in your school.

Tiered Assignment: Mean, Median, Mode, and Range

Overview: These tiered activities provide students with the opportunity to apply their knowledge of and skill with mean, median, mode, and range as they work with lists of data. It is assumed that these assignments will be offered after instruction of these concepts is completed. Thus, these activities can serve as an assessment of students' understanding and skill related to statistics. Students may work independently or in cooperative learning groups to complete the tasks, with the teacher making that determination. Teachers may allow the use of calculators for each tier.

Standards:
- Calculate, use, and interpret the mean, median, mode, and range for a set of data
- Create and solve problems involving the measures of central tendency (mean, median, mode) and the range of a set of data

Objectives:

The students will **KNOW**
- The mean of a number set is the sum of the numbers, divided by the total number of numbers in the set.
- The median of a number set is the middle value of the set.
- The procedure for determining the median differs depending on whether there is an odd or even number of number in the set.
- The mode of a number set is the most frequent value found in the set (the number which appears most often).
- A set can have more than one mode or no mode at all.
- The range of a set of numbers is the largest value in the set minus the smallest value in the set.

The students will **UNDERSTAND THAT**
- The mean, median, mode, and range form patterns and relationships.
- Appropriate statistical methods can be selected and used to analyze data.
- Data must be organized by listing values from smallest to largest in order to determine the mead, median, mode, and range.

The students will **BE ABLE TO**
- Organize data to calculate the mean, median, mode, and range.
- Use a variety of graphical methods to display, organize and interpret data.
- Make inferences and predictions based on analysis of a set of data.
- Use the mean, median, mode and range to create and solve problems.

Basis for Differentiation: Student readiness with regard to:
- mastery of mean, median, mode, and range
- structure versus open-endedness
- defined versus fuzzy problem

Tier One = lower readiness

Note to the teacher: Students will need access to a variety of basketball box scores. The box scores are compiled for each game and list each player on the team and how many points that player scored during the game.

If it is basketball season, these can be obtained from the local newspaper. If basketball is not in season, these statistics are posted on-line. Type "basketball box scores" into your search engine and a variety of sites will provide this information. Students may select a favorite team for this activity.

In reality, most sports in the newspaper provide statistics which could be compiled into a list of data, e.g. listing the points scored by each local football team who played a game on a given weekend. In the following directions, just substitute the sport addressed for basketball box scores.

Tier Two = middle readiness

Tier Three = higher readiness

Math

Tier One

This activity involves the use of basketball box scores. Your teacher will either provide you with box scores from the newspaper or tell you how to find them on-line. The box scores are compiled for every game and list each player on the team. Beside the player's name is a number that shows how many points that player scored during the game.

Make a list of the points scored by each player. This list will form your data. Choose teams that are favorites of yours or ones that appeal to you. Select the box scores for five games of your choice and make a list of the points scored.

Calculate the mean, median, mode, and range for each game.

Tier Two

Use the topics from the list below and conduct a survey of students in your class or school. Collect data from 15-20 students. Ask each student all five of the questions. Design a chart to help you organize the data as you collect it.
- How many people live in your house on a regular basis?
- How many letters are in your first and last name?
- How many pens, pencils, or markers do you have with you at school today?
- About how many hours do you watch TV in a week?
- About how many sodas do you drink in a week, including soda in a cup, bottle, or can?

Make five lists of the numbers collected for each of the five questions. Calculate the mean, median, mode, and range for the data involved in the responses to each question,

----

Tier Three

For this activity you are assuming the role of a statistician, a person who collects and analyzes data. Your first job is to explore the website "The World Almanac for Kids" (www.worldalmanacforkids.com/explore/index.html). This site is filled with a wide variety of data lists. Spend time finding subjects that you feel would be of interest to students at your grade level. Select five different subjects that generate lists of data, each one containing 10-15 numbers.

Use these lists to create 5 problems that practice calculating the mean, median, mode, and range of the numbers. Give clear directions that will be easily understood and include the data lists that will be needed to solve each problem.

Other students will then be given the opportunity to solve the problems that you designed.

Tiered Assignment: Measurement

Overview: These tiered activities provide students with the opportunity to work with the U.S. customary and metric systems of measurement in situations where estimation of the solution is required. It is assumed that these assignments will be offered after instruction of the measurement skills is completed. Students may work independently or in similar-readiness, cooperative learning groups to complete the tasks, with the teacher making that determination.

Standards:
- Compare units of measure for length, weight/mass, and volume within the U.S. customary system and the metric system
- Estimate conversions between units in each system
- Estimate and then determine length, weight/mass, and liquid volume/capacity using standard and metric units of measure

Objectives:
The students will **KNOW**
- The names for standard and metric units of measure for length, weight/mass and liquid volume.
- The context of the measurement problem will determine which unit is appropriate for expressing the measured value, e.g. measuring the distance between home and school would be best expressed in miles or kilometers as opposed to feet and meters.

The students will **UNDERSTAND THAT**
- Both standard and metric measures are encountered in real-life measurement situations in the United States.
- Ballpark comparisons can be used to estimate conversions between standard and metric units of measure in lieu of memorizing conversion factors.
- Estimating measurements is a life skill that is pervasive and on-going in the real world.

The students will **BE ABLE TO**
- Name standard and metric units of measure for length, weight/mass, and volume.
- Analyze a measurement problem to determine the appropriate unit of measure to use.
- Make ballpark comparisons to estimate conversion between standard and metric measurement units.
- Evaluate a measurement problem to estimate its measured answer.

Basis for Differentiation: Student readiness with regard to:
- mastery of measurement skills
- ability to participate in open-ended, divergent thinking
- abstractness

Tier One = lower readiness *Note to the teacher: You may want to bring in a collection of items from home if your classroom does not provide enough variety for this activity.*

Tier Two = middle readiness *Note to the teacher: This activity requires the use of a bathroom scale. You may want to bring in a collection of items from home if your classroom does not provide enough variety for this activity.*

Tier Three = higher readiness

Math

Tier One

Choose 10 very different items around the classroom. These items might come from your backpack, the shelves and counters in the room, or they might be selected from items that your teacher has brought into the classroom specifically for this lesson. The items can have a regular shape, such as a square or rectangle, but they can also be irregular in shape. Try to select objects that vary in size.

Your job is to estimate the length of each object twice from end to end. Make one of your estimations using a metric unit of measure and another using a standard unit of measure. You must decide which unit is appropriate for each object. Before making your estimations, use measuring tools to observe the size of an inch, foot, centimeter, meter, etc., to use as a basis for estimating. Once your estimations are complete, use the measurement tools to measure the actual length of each object.

Construct a chart to record your estimates and actual measures. Calculate the difference between the two and indicate whether each estimate was too long or too short. Record this information on your chart. Give your chart to your teacher when it is completed.

- -

Tier Two

Choose 10 very different items around the classroom. These items might come from your backpack, the shelves and counters in the room, or they might be selected from items that your teacher has brought into the classroom specifically for this lesson. Try to select items that vary in size.

Your job is to estimate the weight of each object in pounds. Before attempting your estimations, select an eleventh item to serve as your control. Weigh this item using the scales provided by your teacher and hold it to get an idea of what that weight feels like. Hold each of your ten items separately and compare its weight to the feel of holding your control item, whose weight you know. Use this comparison to estimate each object's weight in pounds. Once your estimations are complete, use the scale to determine the actual weight of each object.

Construct a chart to record your estimates and actual measures. Calculate the difference between the two and indicate whether each estimate was too heavy or too light. The conversion factor for changing pounds into kilograms is 0.454, which means an object's weight in kilograms is a little less than one half its weight in pounds. Using this information, and knowing the actual weight of the objects, estimate each object's weight in kilograms and record this information on your chart.

Give your chart to your teacher when it is completed.

Tier Three

How much water do you drink in a year? Would this amount fill a bathtub? Would it fill a swimming pool?

Your task is to design a method of estimating how much water the members of your class drink in one year. What data would you need to collect from the students? Would a survey be needed? If so, what questions would you ask?

Once you have designed a plan, put it into action. Collect the needed information from the other students in the class. Explain that they only need to estimate their daily intake of water. Remember, 8 oz. = 1 cup, 8 cups = 1 quart and 4 quarts = 1 gallon. The conversion factor for changing gallons into liters is 4.55, which means the liquid volume in a gallon holds about 4 1/2 liters. Determine your class's yearly amount of drinking water in both gallons and liters.

Share your results with the class.

Tiered Assignment: Ratio and Proportion

Overview: These tiered activities provide students with the opportunity to work in hands-on, engaging ways while demonstrating their understanding of and skill with ratio and proportion. These tasks should follow instruction and practice with these concepts. Students may work on these independently or in similar-readiness groups or pairs as determined by the teacher.

Standards:
- Describe and compare two sets of data using ratios
- Use three appropriate notations to express ratio
- Interpret and use ratios in different contexts
- Develop and use ratio and proportion to solve problems

Objectives:
The students will **KNOW**
- A ratio is a comparison of two numbers.
- Ratios can be expressed in three different formats.
- To compare ratios, they should be written as fractions.
- A proportion is a statement that two ratios are equal.

The students will **UNDERSTAND THAT**
- A ratio can be expressed in simplest terms, just as a fraction can be reduced.
- A ratio expresses the same comparison, regardless of the format in which it is written.
- Proportions can be used to solve practical problems when a value is unknown.
- Values within a proportion must be expressed in the same unit in order to solve the proportion correctly.

The students will **BE ABLE TO**
- Express compared values as ratios using three different formats.
- Compare ratios.
- Simplify ratios.
- Solve problems that utilize ratio.

Basis for Differentiation: Student readiness with regard to:
- skill with ratios and proportions
- complexity

Tier One = lower readiness
Note to the teacher: Students will need individual packages of M & M's (or other candy that is packaged in various colors, such as Skittles) for this activity. Peer partner groups are recommended for this tier. Students may donate the candy.

Tier Two = higher readiness

Note to the teacher: Cooperative learning groups are recommended for this tier.

You will need to purchase or have students donate five or six bags of individually wrapped candy/granola bars/Rice Krispie squares, etc. The goal is to have a variety of food products. The price for each bag should be clearly marked. If there is no price tag on the bag, use a marker to denote price. If students donate, they must remember the cost of the food. The groups working on this activity will be sharing bags of individually wrapped treats/food.

The first task is to record the total cost of each bag. Each group then opens several bags and counts the individual pieces of food in each bag. Share this information with all groups so that each student knows the cost of each bag as well as how many items were in each.

The teacher will then **randomly** *divide the individual pieces from the bags among groups. No group will get an equal amount of the same type of food.*

Math

Tier One

Open your package of candy and spread the pieces out on a paper towel or clean sheet of paper. Sort the candy into piles according to color.

Your job is to compare the number of pieces in the color piles by expressing the comparison as ratios. You will express each ratio in the three different formats that were introduced in class. If the ratio can be simplified, reduce the comparison to lowest terms. Include both comparisons that can be made between two colors. For example, you should express the ratio of red pieces to green pieces **and** the ratio of green pieces to red pieces. Be sure to compare the pieces of each color to every other color in the pack.

Once you have completed describing all of the ratios possible, compare your results with a partner to discover similarities and differences in color combinations between packages.

- -

Tier Two

Your first task is to name ratios as fractions that compare the number of each food item in your group to the total number of pieces in the package. Express these ratios in simplest form; reduce the values if necessary.

Your next job is to design proportion problems that will allow you to determine the cost of an individual item as compared to the cost of the entire bag.

Once you have calculated the cost of one piece of each type of food, compare your ratios and your cost per item to other groups' information. Your per-item cost should be the same in all groups.

RAFT: Fractions, Decimals, and Percents

Overview: These RAFT assignments give students an opportunity to show their knowledge of the interrelationships among common fractions, decimal fractions, and percents. Students may complete their assigned tasks either individually or in similar-readiness pairs. The tasks are listed in order of difficulty with the first being the most difficult.

Standards:
- Describe equivalence relationships among common fractions, decimals, and percents
- Develop meaning for percents
- Convert fractions to decimals to percents and vice-versa

Objectives:
The students will **KNOW**
- The relationships that equate fractions, decimals, and percents.

The students will **UNDERSTAND THAT**
- A given mathematical situation or problem would be better served/solved by knowing whether to express amounts as fractions, decimals, or percents.
- Any fractional quantity may be expressed as a common fraction, a decimal fraction, or a percent.
- All three representations of an amount – fraction, decimal, and percent – have their own unique use in the real world.

The students will **BE ABLE TO**
- Compare and order fractions, decimals, and percents.
- Convert an amount into its fractional, decimal, or percentage equivalence.

Basis for Differentiation: Student readiness with regard to:
- the understanding of equivalence relationships among common fractions, decimals, and percents
- abstractness

Fractions, Decimals, and Percents

ROLE	AUDIENCE	FORMAT	TOPIC
Newspaper Reporter	Readers of the newspaper	Questionnaire (of real-life number values)	In the Following Situations, Would You Choose a Fraction, Decimal, or Percentage to Discuss These Amounts?
Common Fractions	Decimals	Letter of complaint	In Today's Technological World, I Get No Respect, Thanks to You
Percents	Humans	Advertisement	Just Look at All the Ways You Use Me in Your Lives!
Math Teacher	Students in a math class	Poster	Methods to Change Fractions to Decimals to Percents and Vice-Versa

RAFT: Geometric Measurement

Overview: These RAFT assignments give students an opportunity to apply their knowledge of perimeter, area, volume, and surface area of two and three-dimensional objects. Students may complete their chosen tasks either individually or with partners of similar readiness. The tasks are listed in order of difficulty with the first being the most difficult.

Standards:
- Determine if a problem situation involving polygons represents the application of perimeter or area
- Determine if a problem situation involving a three-dimensional solid represents the application of surface area or volume.
- Recognize and name of given polygons and 3-dimensional solids

Objectives:
The students will **KNOW**
- The difference between two and three-dimensional objects.
- The purpose for calculating perimeter, area, surface area, and volume.

The students will **UNDERSTAND THAT**
- Perimeter, area, volume and surface area are affected by changes in scale.
- Each of the measures of perimeter, area, volume, and surface area address different applications in the real world.

The students will **BE ABLE TO**
- Calculate the perimeter, area, volume, and surface area of given two and three-dimensional objects.
- Analyze a problem to discern whether perimeter, area, volume, or surface area is required to produce a correct solution.

Basis for Differentiation: Student readiness with regard to:
- the understanding of geometric measures
- complexity
- foundational versus transformational

Geometric Measurement

ROLE	AUDIENCE	FORMAT	TOPIC
Math Teacher	Math students	A Mini Book of Problems	Word Problems Which Utilize Perimeter, Area, Volume, and Surface Area (Two problems for each, with an answer key at the end.)
Quadrilaterals	The World	A User's Handbook	Real-world Reasons to Determine Our Area and Perimeter
Area	Surface Area	A Conversation	Ways in Which You and I Are Used by Humans
3-Dimensional Solids	Polygons	Venn Diagram	We Have Our Likenesses and Differences

RAFT: Positive and Negative Rational Numbers

Overview: These RAFT assignments give students an opportunity to apply their knowledge and understanding of positive and negative rational numbers. Each student may choose which task he or she wants to complete and may work on it either individually or with a partner.

Standards:
- Develop number sense for negative rational numbers
- Compare and order positive and negative rational numbers

Objectives:
The students will **KNOW**
- The properties of rational numbers expressed in a variety of forms.

The students will **UNDERSTAND THAT**
- Every rational number can be expressed as either a terminating or repeating decimal.
- Every positive rational number has an opposite negative rational number.

The students will **BE ABLE TO**
- Differentiate between rational and irrational numbers.
- Use a number line to compare and order positive and negative rational numbers.

Basis for Differentiation: Student learning profile (Gardner's Multiple Intelligences)

Positive and Negative Rational Numbers

ROLE	AUDIENCE	FORMAT	TOPIC
A Positive Rational Number	Negative rational numbers	A Poem Expressing Affection	We Complement Each Other Nicely
Rational Numbers	Irrational Numbers	Song Lyrics (set to a melody of your choice)	If You Knew Fractions Like We Know Fractions
A Negative Rational Number	The Human Race	A Guide Book	Where to Find Negative Values in the Real World (*Example: the number of feet traveled underground to dig a well*)
Guidance Counselor	Student	Counseling session	Is Your Personality More Like a Positive or a Negative Number? (*Explain your answer using several examples*)

Think-Tac-Toe: Probability

Overview: These Think-Tac-Toe options allow students to choose their own ways of showing what they have come to know and understand about probability and its applications in the real world. The tasks are structured to address student interest and personal choice. Students may choose any three options going across, down or diagonally within the grid. This Think-Tac-Toe can be used as one of the culminating activities for a unit on probability and can be combined with other formal assessments to evaluate student learning.

Standards:
- Analyze problem situations and make predictions, using knowledge of probability
- Use a sample space to determine the probability of an event
- Conduct experiments involving simple and compound events
- Design and conduct experiments to solve problems
- Investigate and describe the difference between the probability of an event found through simulation versus the theoretical probability of that same event

Objectives:
The students will **KNOW**
- Conducting a probability experiment can simulate theoretical results.
- Probability can be expressed as a fraction or a percentage.
- Probability is inherent in the natural and man-made world.

The students will **UNDERSTAND THAT**
- The actual probability of an event does not always equal the theoretical probability of an event.
- Data can be used to estimate the probability of future events.
- The larger the number of samples in a simulated experiment, the more likely the chance that the result approximates the theoretical probability.

The students will **BE ABLE TO**
- Conduct a probability experiment.
- Predict the probability of future events.
- Determine and compare experimental and theoretical probabilities for simple and compound events.
- Design a probability experiment and conduct it to solve a problem.

Basis for Differentiation: Student interest and personal choice

Note to the teacher: The answer to the last problem in the grid concerning the lottery is 1/1,906,884. Each time a numbered ball is drawn, it reduces the number of balls that pop up. The solution is reached by multiplying 5/49 x 4/48 x 3/47 x 2/46 x1/45, and reducing the answer. For students unfamiliar with how lottery numbers are picked, you may need to explain the process for this activity to be correctly analyzed.

Think-Tac-Toe: Probability

Select a novel of your choice and turn to a random page. Tally the number of times each letter of the alphabet appears on the page, designing a chart to record the data. Add up the totals for each letter and the grand total of letters on the page. Use a calculator to determine the percentage probability of finding each letter. Record all data on your chart. Report to the class the top ten letters that occurred and the bottom five letters. If you were a player on "Wheel of Fortune" what advice does this survey give you?	Theoretically, tossing a coin gives you a 1/2 chance of tossing a head or a tail. Test this probability. Toss a coin 100 times and record whether you tossed a head or a tail. Determine the probability of your experiment. How close were you to the theoretical probability? Would a larger number of tosses have gotten you closer? Why or why not?	Conduct a survey of 75 people, recording their birthdays. Design a chart to collect and record the data. The people you survey can be students, teachers, family members, neighbors, etc. Using your data, what is the probability that: 2 people have the same birthday? a person has the same birthday as yours? Using your data, estimate the probability of child being born in May during the up-coming year.
A rider is participating in a moun-tain biking race whose route crosses a variety of terrain. The path comes to a fork, with one choice being significantly shorter than the other. However, the rider has a 4/1 chance of blowing a tire on the shorter route than on the longer route. Create a picture of both routes, indicating why the one has a 4/1 probability of popping a tire over the other. Which route should the rider choose and why? Include this written response with your picture.	Use a pair of regular dice. Roll the dice 100 times and record how many times you roll a double 1, a double 2, a double 3, a double 4, a double 5, and a double 6. Do not record any of the throws that don't produce doubles. Express the probability of rolling each of the six possibilities of producing a double throw as fractions. What is the probability of rolling any set of doubles? How would you predict board game makers would use this information when designing the rules of their games?	Using a deck of playing cards, what is the probability of drawing a face card (Jack, Queen, or King) from the deck? Conduct an experiment to determine how close you come to this theoretical probability. Shuffle the cards 50 different times and have a partner or yourself draw one card after each shuffle. Record the number of times a face card is drawn and calculate your actual probability. How close were you to the theoretical probability?
Based on your observation alone, predict the probability a student in your school wears glasses or contacts. Conduct a survey of 50 students in your school to determine how many do or do not wear contacts/glasses. Calculate the probabil-ity of wearing contacts/glasses and not wearing them. Express the results as a fraction and a percentage. You may use a calculator. Would you recom-mend that an eye doctor move into your school's attendance zone? Why or why not?	The probability of being struck by lightning is 1/600,000. We are bom-barded with probabilities such as this from many different walks of life. Using your search engine and the Internet, research at least six other interesting probabilities that apply to our lives. Share these with the rest of your class, along with a paragraph that describes what, if any, effects these probabilities have on your life.	Many states have a lottery today to raise money for important causes. Much of this money is given to education within the state. The most popular game has a player pick five numbers from the sequence 1-49. If the player's numbers match the five drawn in any order, then the player wins a great deal of money. Design a method to determine what the probability is of winning this type of lottery. (Hint: multiplication is involved)

Complex Instruction: Properties of Operations with Real Numbers

Overview: These complex instruction tasks invite students to work in learning profile-based groups of three or four while examining the properties of operations that assist in simplifying algebraic expressions. Each task focuses on the students' understanding of the assigned property and their ability to apply it in new settings. It is assumed that these tasks will be assigned after instruction of the unit is completed. Therefore, these tasks can serve as part of the final assessment for the unit.

Standards:
- Identify and apply the following properties of operations:
    - The commutative property for addition and multiplication
    - The additive and multiplicative identity properties
    - The associative properties for addition and multiplication
    - The additive and multiplicative inverse properties
    - The distributive property
    - Order of operations

Objectives:
The students will **KNOW**
- The properties of operations (listed above).
- The uses of the properties of operations to simplify algebraic expressions.

The students will **UNDERSTAND THAT**
- These properties are used to verify the results of solving algebraic equations.
- These properties hold true for all operations with rational numbers.
- The order of operations is essential to computing chains of calculations.
- These properties govern the manner in which mathematicians all over the world justify their manipulation of rational numbers.

The students will **BE ABLE TO**
- State and express algebraically the properties of operations.
- Recognize each property of operations when it is utilized to simplify expressions and solve equations.
- Apply the properties of operations in unique settings.

Basis for Differentiation: Student learning profile (Gardner's Multiple Intelligences) with some flexibility to address readiness issues with abstract versus concrete thinking

----

📄 **Directions**   Work in your group to complete each of the tasks. The tasks each require different abilities and skills so spend time deciding who will take the lead on each task. However, as a group, you are responsible for completing all of the tasks.

Planning is crucial. Who will be the leader for each task? Who will work on each task? How will you help one another?

Your final products should be neat, accurate, detailed, and they should be thoughtful and demonstrate fully your understanding of your assigned property.

Math

Task One (the wordsmith, verbal/linguistic)

Order of operations allows us to perform strings of calculations following rules that assist everyone in reaching the same answer. The order in which we complete the calculations states that we:

- Perform all operations inside parentheses, if they are present.
- Simplify all exponents, working from left to right.
- Perform all multiplications and divisions, working from left to right.
- Perform all additions and subtractions, working from left to right.

The standard mnemonic device that is used to help us remember this order is **P**lease **E**xcuse **M**y **D**ear **A**unt **S**ally (Parentheses, Exponents, Multiplication, Division, Addition, and Subtraction).

Your task is to create two new mnemonic devices that will help your classmates remember this order. Try to make them appropriately modern and relevant to today's teenagers. Then create two problems that can be solved using your new phrases so that the other students in the class can practice using your creations.

Task Two (the reflective thinker, intrapersonal)

The identity properties for addition and multiplication describe operations which, when performed on a number, allow it to keep its same identity once the operation is over. Thus, $A + 0$ will always equal A, regardless of what value A assumes, and $B \times 1$ will always equal B, regardless of what value B assumes.

We all have our own unique identity, and we are resistant to the forces in the world that try to change us. In our real lives, our true friends and family are our identity elements, just like 0 and 1: they accept us for who we are and don't try to change us.

Create a conversation between 0 and 1 in which they are discussing why it is important for numbers to have an identity element. Think of when and why you use the identity property as you write the dialogue. Give the numbers human qualities and allow 0 and 1 to explain why they play such an important role in the world of numbers.

Task Three (the artist, visual/spatial)

The distributive property is essential to simplifying expressions so that equations can be solved. Associating the parentheses with multiplication and then removing them is confusing to many students. Study the algebraic representation of the distributive property, $a(b + c) = ab + ac$.

Create a visual format to help explain this property, using either numbers or variables as the central elements. You may give them human characteristics, and then draw a comic strip or a story board. It might show, for example, A, carrying a large pizza, meeting up with two others, B and C, and then sharing that pizza with them. Regardless of your format, create some type of visual scene that will explain the distributive property to other students. Be ready to share your product with the class.

Complex Instruction: Properties of Two-Dimensional Plane Figures

Overview: These complex instruction tasks allow students to work in learning profile-based groups of four or five while examining the properties of a variety of two-dimensional plane figures. Each task focuses on the students' understanding of the assigned shapes and their relevance to math and the real world. It is assumed that these tasks will be assigned after instruction of the unit is completed. Thus, as culminating assignments for the unit, these tasks can be used as part of the unit assessment.

Standards:
- Identify, classify, and describe the characteristics of plane figures, describing their similarities, differences, and defining properties
- Compare and contrast the following quadrilaterals: parallelogram, rectangle, square, rhombus, and trapezoid
- Identify and draw the following polygons: pentagon, hexagon, heptagon, octagon, nonagon, and decagon
- Identify the radius, diameter, chord, center, and circumference of a circle
- Determine the congruence of polygons by direct comparison, given their attributes
- Identify and define a plane

Objectives:
The students will **KNOW**
- The distinguishing characteristics of different quadrilaterals.
- Polygons are recognizable by the number of sides that form them.
- The determining factors that separate congruent and non-congruent figures.

The students will **UNDERSTAND THAT**
- Plane figures differ from solid figures by the number of dimensions they possess.
- The number of sides and angles that comprise a plane figure sets it apart from all other plane figures.
- A circle differs from all other plane figures because of its lack of straight edges.
- Plane figures surround us in the real world.

The students will **BE ABLE TO**
- Identify plane figures and describe their distinguishing characteristics.
- Distinguish between congruent and non-congruent figures.
- Draw a given two-dimensional shape.

Basis for Differentiation: Student learning profile (Gardner's Multiple Intelligences) with some flexibility to address readiness issues with abstract versus concrete thinking

---

Directions   Work in your group to complete each of the tasks. The tasks each require different abilities and skills so spend time deciding who will take the lead on each task. However, as a group, you are responsible for completing all of the tasks.

Planning is crucial. Who will be the leader for each task? Who will work on each task? How will you help one another? Your final products should be neat, accurate, detailed, and thoughtful and demonstrate fully your understanding of plane figures and their characteristics.

Math

Task One (mathematical/logical)

What is a plane? We cannot understand plane figures until we understand the concept of a plane.

Your task is to assume the role of a math teacher. Research the characteristics of a plane. How can you help others understand a concept that is central to an entire branch of geometry? How do plane figures differ from 3-dimensional shapes?

Design a mini-lesson that will answer these questions for the rest of the class. You may use visuals and props in your lesson. Your goal is to provide a thorough understanding of a plane's characteristics.

- -

Task Two (visual/spatial)

Posters, posters, posters!

Your task is to create posters with visual representations of plane figures, beginning with a 3-sided plane figure and adding a side each time until you reach a 10-sided figure. For the four-sided figure, draw a generic quadrilateral. Another group will be studying the special kinds of quadrilaterals. Your task will be completed when you have finished eight posters. Label each shape with its name and the number of sides and angles it has.

You may be as creative as you like in designing your posters as long as the shapes are mathematically accurate. Visually stunning is your goal!

- -

Task Three (verbal linguistic/visual spatial)

Quadrilaterals are the most common shapes found in man-made structures. The different types of quadrilaterals have special characteristics that set them apart.

Your task is to create a conversation/dialogue involving a rectangle, a parallelogram, a square, a rhombus, and a trapezoid. This conversation should focus on how these shapes are different and how they are alike. It should also address how these shapes are used in the world of mathematics and in the real world. Your dialogue may be humorous, but it must be mathematically accurate.

You will each take a role and read the dialogue to the rest of the class. Recruit another student to help in the presentation if there are not enough members in your group to pair up with each shape.

Task Four (bodily/kinesthetic)

The circle stands apart in the world of two-dimensional plane figures. Its continuous curved form has fascinated humans for thousands of years.

Your task is to assist the class in understanding vocabulary unique to the circle. You will accomplish this task by using your bodies to explain the radius, diameter, chord, center, and circumference of a circle. You may also use string, yarn, or other props necessary to reach your goal. Design body formations that will explain the important characteristics of the circle. You may connect the formations together in the form of a dance if you prefer. Title cards or verbal dialogue should describe what your bodies are forming.

This is a chance to let creativity combine with math to produce a memorable lesson about the circle.

- -

Task Five (intrapersonal/verbal linguistic/visual spatial)

Congruent figures are just like identical twins: you cannot tell them apart. Research congruency to discover the attributes that must exist for figures to be called congruent.

Your task is then to assume the role of a congruent shape and to reflect on how it must feel to be exactly like another figure (similar to having an identical twin). Compose a journal entry describing the feelings of congruent shapes, knowing that it is impossible to distinguish them from any other shape to which they are congruent. You may give human characteristics to your shapes as you reflect on their feelings. Include in your journal entry drawings of several different pairs of congruent figures, along with labels indicating why they are congruent.

You might want to divide your group into smaller subgroups so that more than one journal entry is produced. Share your product with the rest of the class.

Chapter 6: Science

Tiered Assignments: Cell Biology

Overview: This tiered project is designed to come at the end of a unit on cell biology. The basis for differentiation centers on students with varying levels of understanding and comfort with the materials, from a relatively simple analysis of cell parts and their functions to how the more complicated processes of cells are affected by the external factors. The current issue of the avian bird flu is used as the basis for this problem-based, whole class review of cell biology.

Standards:
- Describe the structure of a cell, its parts, and their functions
- Compare and contrast a variety of microbes to cite how they affect the ability of these cell parts to function properly
- Assess how humans can act to mitigate the spread of disease in the external population

Objectives:
The students will **KNOW**
- Key terminology associated with an in-depth study of cell biology.
- Functions of identified cell structures.
- Types of external factors that adversely affect the health of healthy cells.
- Specific means by which diseases spread, both internally and externally.

The students will **UNDERSTAND THAT**
- While diseases may be caused by a number of factors, they typically just affect cells in one of several fundamental ways.
- Diseases spread in an environment when that environment is conducive to their growth.
- Factors can be put in place to limit the growth of diseases.
- Cells have built-in features designed to keep functioning properly, but disease agents attack the function of these parts.

The students will **BE ABLE TO**
- Describe the effect on cells of diseases caused by microscopic biological hazards.
- Evaluate human attempts to reduce the risk of and treatments for microbial infections.
- Analyze data to find trends or patterns to determine how an infectious disease may spread.

Basis for Differentiation: Student readiness with regard to foundational understanding versus complex, transformational understanding

---

Group One (lower readiness)
Group Two (middle readiness)
Group Three (higher readiness)

Note to the Teacher: The basis for this cooperative, tiered learning activity rests on the current global concern about the potential for an avian bird flu pandemic on a massive scale. To help make this relevant for the students in the class, it is suggested that the teacher bring in newspaper clippings or other forms of current events news. An expert from the medical field might also be called upon to make a short introductory presentation about this disease. To be authentic, the result of this project should ideally be presented to a group of other students or adults. It would be ideal, also, to find someone who is an expert in some way in the field of medicine (a doctor, health care administrator, school nurse, EMT, etc). A "real audience" would allow for students to receive authentic feedback about the effectiveness of their plans.

There is no reason why a teacher, if he or she is uncomfortable with this particular choice of disease, could not choose to do the same activity with an entirely different disease (This is important to keep in mind if the issue of bird flu itself becomes outdated or less relevant in some other way.). Similarly, all other aspects of this project are open to change. If there are other terms that the teacher wants the class to review, add them! If the teacher feels the project is too large then he or she can adjust the amount of material being covered or break a larger task into smaller ones by reassigning key portions to other groups. Three groups are suggested here to aid the teacher in thinking about how to differentiate – there could certainly be two or three groups working simultaneously at each level.

- -

📄 The Assignment
Background for ALL Students

There has been a tremendous amount of discussion, debate, and worry expressed in the news about the potential of a bird flu pandemic hitting the United States. There have been television mini-series, night reports on the news, and calls across the nation for cities to form crisis plans. The result is a lot of confusion and misinformation about what exactly the bird flu is. Our job is to correct any misunderstandings. To accomplish this rather large feat, we will divide the class into three groups. Each group will have a specific task that is important to the end result, which is a presentation to a large group. This group will help us evaluate our findings and presentation.

All groups should read the assigned tasks thoroughly. Be sure that each group member understands what the group's responsibility is, and then assign the tasks so that each piece of the assignment is addressed and so that each member has something to work on. It is up to your group to decide how you will best present the information to your audience, but you should have a good, strong visual as a means of anchoring your presentation. You may decide to use posters, Power Point, or even a small interactive skit to explain your ideas. The means by which you convey the information is up to you.

Before you begin working on your finals products, your ideas should be presented to the teacher for approval.

Science

Group One

At a most basic level, the avian bird flu harms people by affecting the health of their cells. The audience will need to know a great deal more about these fundamental building blocks and the "things" that can affect their health. Your task is to give the audience a thorough understanding of this essential information – without it, they will be lost. Don't worry about trying to relate this information to the bird flu; your task is to give the audience a short biology lesson on cells.

Using class notes, the textbook, reputable internet websites, and other materials, create a presentation the gives the answers to the following questions:

- What does a healthy human cell look like? Describe its **size** and **shape**.
- What are the basic **structures of a cell** and what essential functions does each part accomplish? Be sure to mention the **mitochondria, nucleus, cell wall, cytoplasm**, and **vacuoles**.
- How does a healthy cell get the energy it needs to stay alive?

Your presentation MUST include the bold words listed in the questions above. Part of your grade will be based on your use of these words in the actual presentation.

Group Two

The avian bird flu is tricky for doctors to deal with, partly because it is a virus, not a bacteria. Both, however, are harmful to cells. Your job is to build on the information provided by the first group to help the audience now understand what happens when a healthy cell is attacked. Don't worry about trying to relate this information to the bird flu; your task is to give the audience a short biology lesson on the hazards that cells face.

You should use your class notes, the textbook, reputable internet websites, and other materials to answer the following questions and create your presentation.

- In general terms, what factors affect the health of a cell?
- What, exactly, is a **virus**? How is it different from a **bacteria** or a **parasite**?
- How do viruses and bacteria harm cells to cause **disease**? (Be sure to explain how they interact with or affect the various parts of a cell.)
- What do we mean by **carriers** of disease?

Your presentation MUST include the bold words listed in the questions above. Part of your grade will be based on your use of these words in the actual presentation.

Group Three

The previous two groups have set the stage for you. They have explained what healthy cells are like and how they are negatively affected by external factors. Your group's task is to specifically address the avian bird flu. To do this, develop your presentation around the following questions. You should use reputable internet websites and other relevant materials to create your presentation.

- How does a virus that originates in a bird population make the transfer to humans? (What is a **mutagen**?)
- If there is an outbreak, what are the **vectors** of its growth?
- How might stockpiling and administering a **vaccine** help control the harm of the flu?
- How does vaccine work in the human body?

Your presentation MUST include the bold words listed in the questions above. Part of your grade will be based on your use of these words in the actual presentation. Furthermore, be sure to include the latest, relevant information available on the bird flu including how many cases have been noted to date, where they have occurred, and where scientists predict the flu will hit next.

Tiered Assignments: Solar System

Overview: These tiered solar system projects provide students with the opportunity to review a wide variety of topics typically included in a study of the solar system. Students may work in small cooperative learning groups to develop and carry out the project, or they may work to complete them independently. This is for the teacher to decide.

Standards:
- Analyze the components and cycles of the solar system including the sun, planets and moons, asteroids and meteors, comets, phases, seasons, day/year, and eclipses
- Describe the unique features of Earth that make it especially favorable to fostering life

Objectives:
The students will **KNOW**
- The names of each planet.
- The key characteristics that distinguish the planets from one another, specifically the types of atmosphere, their relative distances from the sun, the numbers of associated moons, and the planets' structural compositions.

The students will **UNDERSTAND THAT**
- The Earth, due to its structural composition, ready presence of water, and unique atmospheric qualities, is exceptionally suited to support human life.
- The ability for a creature to live in any given environment is dependent upon that creature's ability to adapt to its unique environment.

The students will **BE ABLE TO**
- Compare and contrast the Earth to other planets in terms of size, composition, relative distance from the sun, and the ability to support life.
- Evaluate their current understandings/knowledge of the planets that compose our solar system.

Basis for Differentiation: Student readiness with regard to:
- Structure versus open-endedness
- Concreteness versus abstractness
- Content intricacy (simple versus complex)

Note to the Teacher: Below are general suggestions for culminating projects for a unit on the solar system. It is essential that every student feel that he or she is getting a chance to do an engaging and stimulating activity. For this reason, the general project suggestions are the same for all students. What differentiates the three levels is:

- *the content itself*
- *the complexity of the projects' requirements, as decided by the teacher*

Suggestions for these possible modifications are listed with each project description, but it is, of course, up to the teacher, to decide upon these details. In all cases, the teacher, in an effort to make sure all of the planets are addressed, will assign them to each student.

Differentiation by Content

One of the simplest ways for the teacher to differentiate according to content is to assign a "simpler planet" to a lower-level group and a more "complex" planet to a higher level group. For example, Mercury (essentially an extremely hot, rocky ball with no atmosphere) or Pluto (Mercury's opposite for all intents and purposes) are far less complicated than, say, Venus or Saturn (which have harsh atmospheres or many moons and rings). Note Pluto is no longer considered a planet, so students may choose another "simple" planet.

Similarly, it is safe to say that simply because of technological barriers, scientists have been able to study or gather more data about certain planets. Selecting planets about which we know a great deal (for example, Mars) might be a superb choice for higher-level students, as they must necessarily grapple with more associated data. To this end, lower-level students might be assigned planets about which relatively little data has been collected.

Suggested Planets for Lower Level Thinkers: Mercury, Uranus, (Pluto)
Suggested Planets for Middle Level Thinkers: Earth, Mars, Jupiter
Suggested Planets for Higher Level Thinkers: Venus, Saturn, Neptune

Differentiation by Project Requirements

Another way for the teacher to offer some differentiation at the end of this unit is by offering tasks of varying levels of complexity. The teacher may simply ask lower-level students to tackle the projects, insisting on fewer requirements but each done at a level that demonstrates thorough understanding. Conversely, higher-level students might tackle more of the project requirements, especially those demanding a higher level of sophistication.

Finally, while the suggested projects are oriented towards illustrations, there is no reason a teacher could not turn the same project into a 3-dimensional project like a sculpture or a diorama.

The Project Choices

Can You Picture That?

Imagine you are somehow able to stand on the surface of your assigned planet. (If you are assigned a gas planet, such as Jupiter, you'll have to really use your imagination!)

First, draw a landscape view of what you see as you "sit" there. Be sure to consider all you know about:

- The planet's environment
- Landforms
- Surface composition
- Any other pertinent information that scientists have been able to glean about the planet's surface, including coloration and any other unique features

Second, draw a picture of what you see as you look up into a night sky on your planet. For this, you will need to be sure that you consider what scientists have learned about:

- The planet's atmosphere (Can you even see through it or is it too gassy?)
- Its orbiting moons (Does it have moons? How many?)
- Its distance from the sun (Is it close or far away? How would the sun look from this distance?)

In all cases, be sure that your illustrations, to the best of your ability, reflect correct coloration, relative size, and any other unique understandings we have about your assigned planet.

- -

Create-a-Creature

Your task is to design a creature that could live on your assigned planet. You are allowed to be fanciful in your creation of this creature so that you may, for example, pretend that your creature is able to gain needed nutrients and minerals by eating rocks. But, however imaginative your creature may be, it must still reflect your understanding of what that planet is really like. In order to do this, you will need to make sure you consider the following aspects of your assigned planet:

- What the atmosphere is like
- What the physical environment of the planet is like
- How strong the gravitational pull of the planet is
- What the average day and night temperatures are

Once you have considered the above list, you should compose a picture that represents your creature. Its physical details should reflect what unique qualities it has "adapted" to survive on your planet. Labels with appropriate descriptors will be helpful in showing what special details you provided (for example: "large bones and big muscles" for a creature who lives on Jupiter).

Furthermore, you should place your creature in the context of its environment. Where would it live? Does your planet offer any unique features that would make an especially cozy, favorable home for your creature? Your illustration should reflect this understanding.

Tiered Assignments: Space Exploration

Overview: These tasks allow students to examine the role of current space exploration, its benefits, and, to a lesser degree, its costs. Their work on these tasks follows some whole-class discussion and study of the history of the U.S. space program. Students may work independently or in pairs depending on their preferences. A variety of resources, including appropriate websites, should be made available.

Standard:
- Analyze the spin-off benefits generated by space exploration technology.

Objectives:
The students will **KNOW**
- Some of the spin-off benefits of the space program.

The students will **UNDERSTAND THAT**
- New technology has both benefits and costs.
- New technology can change the way we live.
- There are differing opinions about the importance and value of the U.S. space program.
- Analysis of both benefits and costs is an important step in the decision-making process.

The students will **BE ABLE TO**
- Analyze benefits of the U.S. space program.
- Evaluate the importance of these benefits.
- Communicate to persuade.

Basis for Differentiation: Student readiness with regard to:
- open-endedness
- abstraction
- real-world situations.

Learning profile with regard to students' individual grouping preferences (option to work on own or with partner).

Tier One = lower readiness
Tier Two = middle readiness
Tier Three = higher readiness

Science

Tier One

NASA's work in space has resulted in many unexpected benefits in the lives of people on Earth. Research these benefits in the areas of health and medicine, public safety, transportation, and consumer goods.

Create a chart or thinking map that shows 3-4 benefits in each of these areas.

Then write a paragraph explaining which benefit of the space program is most important to you. Be sure to explain your reasoning thoroughly!

Tier Two

Consider this: What if the U.S. space program and NASA had never been started? How would our lives be different?

Write a story that tells about the day in a life of a person living in the present if space exploration did not exist and had never existed. What would an average person's life be like without it?

Then create a second story that highlights the differences in the person's day brought about by advances created by the space program. It may help to write the second story first. Make sure that the differences between life with and life without space exploration are clear!

Lastly, create a short statement giving your opinion about the benefits and costs of the U.S. space program.

Tier Three

You are a congressional lobbyist working on behalf of the space program. You realize that Congress has some tough budget decisions to make for the future, but you feel strongly that the space program should receive increased funding. Do your research. How much of the current budget does the space program receive? Given that increasing this amount will take away from other important programs, why should the space program receive more funding?

Create a clear, concise (no more than 4 minutes...people are busy!), and convincing argument designed to persuade members of Congress to vote your way. You **must** consider other programs, such as bills and grants that support education, in your argument.

RAFT: Genetics

Overview: These tiered RAFT assignments give students an opportunity to apply their knowledge of the key terms, concepts, and processes typically highlighted in a middle school-level genetics unit. They are listed in order of difficulty, with the first being the most difficult. Students may complete them individually or with partners.

Standards:
- Investigate and understand that organisms reproduce and transmit genetic
- information to new generations
- Utilize appropriate information systems to build an understanding of heredity and genetics

Objectives:
The students will **KNOW**
- Vocabulary: gene, DNA, RNA, recessive trait, dominant trait, bacteria, virus, mutation, zygote.

The students will **UNDERSTAND THAT**
- Genes are units of information.
- Parents transmit genes to their offspring.
- Some medical conditions and diseases are genetic in origin.
- The processes involved in sorting and recombining parents' genetic material create potential variation among offspring.
- Chromosomes contain genetic information which can be categorized as recessive or dominant; the differences between the two determine the expression of genetic traits.

The students will **BE ABLE TO**
- Explain the role of each parent in the transfer of genetic traits.
- Evaluate the role and function of DNA in a human cell, bacteria, or virus.
- Explain the significance of reproduction.
- Summarize the genetic transmittance of disease.

Basis for Differentiation: Student readiness with regard to:
- Knowledge of genetics
- General thinking skills

Genetics

ROLE	AUDIENCE	FORMAT	TOPIC
A cell in the body	DNA	Love Song/Ballad	Why I Need You in My Life
A protein	Messenger RNA	Letter of Complaint	You Are SO Bossy!
Genes from two different repro-ductive cells	The zygote	Debate	Whose genetic material deserves to be dominant or recessive?
A virus	Other viruses	Mutation Instruction Man-ual	How to Cause Problems for a Healthy Cell

RAFT: Hydrosphere

Overview: These RAFT assignments give students an opportunity to apply their knowledge of the hydrosphere, properties of water, and distribution of water across the planet. Students may complete their chosen tasks either individually or with partners.

Standards:
- Analyze the structure of the water cycle
- Evaluate evidence that estuaries contain nutrients, minerals, and dissolved gases that enhance the growth of life forms
- Describe how humans affect the quality of water
- Analyze the importance of wetlands to surrounding landforms

Objectives:
The students will **KNOW**
- The relationship between evaporation and condensation.
- Ways in which humans pollute the Earth's water sources.
- The characteristics and composition of estuaries.
- Reasons why wetlands must be protected.

The students will **UNDERSTAND THAT**
- People's actions influence the surrounding environment that supports their existence.
- The hydrosphere is dependent upon the water cycle to regulate the distribution of water.
- The hydrosphere provides nutrients and protection for a wide variety of life forms.

The students will **BE ABLE TO**
- Identify how human actions impact the hydrosphere.
- Explain the importance of the hydrosphere in fostering and maintaining life on Earth.
- Conduct research.

Basis for Differentiation: Student interest with regard to the various components that comprise the hydrosphere

---

Hydrosphere

ROLE	AUDIENCE	FORMAT	TOPIC
The world's ocean	Earth's human population	Top Ten List	You're Killing Me! – The ten most damaging ways you are polluting my waters
Evaporation	Condensation	Friendly email	Why We Make Such a Great Team
Chesapeake Bay	Mothers of all marine life and water fowl	Advertising brochure	My Waters Provide the Best Nursery on the Planet
Coastal Louisi-ana Wetlands	The City of New Orleans	Newspaper editorial	Without Me, Your City Cannot Survive Another Hurricane

RAFT: Plate Tectonics

Overview: These RAFT options ask students to demonstrate their understandings of plate tectonics while working in accordance with their different learning profiles. Students should have some background information about plate tectonics and geologic activity, through class activities and discussions, prior to selecting and beginning their RAFT activities. In addition to drawing on their prior knowledge, students should be encouraged to use additional resources provided in the classroom. These activities are designed to be completed individually and can serve as an assessment of students' knowledge, understanding, and skill regarding plate tectonics.

Standards:
- Build an understanding of evidence of change or constancy in landforms over time
- Evaluate the forces which shape the lithosphere

Objectives:
The students will **KNOW**
- Vocabulary: lithosphere, asthenosphere, plate, plate boundary, convergent boundary, divergent boundary, transform boundary, magma, earthquake, volcano, trench.

The students will **UNDERSTAND THAT**
- The lithosphere is made up of large, rigid plates.
- These plates move in different directions and at different speeds.
- Plates meet at plate boundaries.
- There are three different types of plate boundaries that cause different geologic activities and features, such as earthquakes, mountains, volcanoes, and trenches.

The students will **BE ABLE TO**
- Explain the theory of plate tectonics.
- Describe, compare, and contrast convergent boundaries, divergent boundaries, and transform boundaries.
- Predict geologic phenomena.

Basis for Differentiation: Student learning profile (Gardner's Multiple Intelligences)

Plate Tectonics

ROLE	AUDIENCE	FORMAT	TOPIC
A realtor	Prospective buyers	Brochure with illustrations and brief written explanations	If you have to buy a house on a plate boundary, here's the one I would suggest and why
Psychologist or therapist	Patients/clients	A graphic organizer (chart)	How relationships are like plate tectonics and how the results of these relationships are the same
The three different plate boundaries	Geologists	A panel discussion	Which of us you should be most worried about and why
Middle school students	First graders	Demonstration (*using tools & kitchen gadgets provided by the teacher & available in the classroom*)	Here's what these tools and gadgets can teach us about plate tectonics and plate boundaries

Think-Tac-Toe: Chemistry

Overview: These Think-Tac-Toe options allow students to choose their own ways of showing what they have come to know and understand about the nature of chemistry and the chemical substances that surround our daily lives. The tasks are structured according to Gardner's Theory of Multiple Intelligences, with each of the eight intelligences being represented. Students may choose any three options going across, down or diagonally within the grid. This Think-Tac-Toe can be used as one of the culminating activities for a unit on chemistry and/or the structure of matter and can be combined with other formal assessments to evaluate student learning.

Standards:
- Build an understanding of chemistry and chemical concepts
- Investigate matter to discover its properties
- Evaluate the periodic chart to recognize the more than 100 elements and to discover that each element has distinct properties and atomic structures
- Discover that all forms of matter are composed of one or more elements
- Identify areas of life in which chemicals play an important role

Objectives:
The students will **KNOW**
- The structure and composition of an atom.
- The states of matter and their relationship to molecular motion.
- Chemical properties that distinguish one element from another.

The students will **UNDERSTAND THAT**
- All matter is made up of atoms.
- Chemicals play an important role in everyday life.
- Substances can be identified based upon their physical and chemical properties.
- All forms of matter are composed of one or more elements.

The students will **BE ABLE TO**
- Conduct research.
- Read and interpret the periodic chart of the elements.
- Determine the solubility of a substance.
- Identify the use and significance of chemicals in everyday life.
- Describe and illustrate atomic structure.
- Interpret the role of molecular motion in determining the state of matter.
- Justify thinking and defend choices.

Basis for Differentiation: Student learning profile (Gardner's Multiple Intelligences)

Think-Tac-Toe: Chemistry

Many of the elements in the Periodic Table were named in ancient times. Research the word origins of elements whose symbols don't relate to their English names. Identify ten elements named by the ancient Greeks and Romans. Create a spreadsheet on your computer to show the element's ancient name, its symbol, and its modern name. *(Verbal/Linguistic)*	Choose at least five elements, compounds, or a combination of the two. Create cartoon characters out of their chemical symbols. Design a comic strip based on your characters and draw enough panels to describe an adventure, based on your knowledge of chemistry concepts. For example, your strip might show how the elements combined to form a compound. *(Visual/Spatial)*	Conduct an interview with a doctor, nurse, or any type of health care professional. You may interview this individual in person, over the phone, via e-mail or instant messaging. Design questions to discover how chemicals might play a part in the following diseases or syndromes: cancer, diabetes, heart disease, birth defects, asthma, learning disorders, and behavior disorders. *(Interpersonal)*
You are a drop of water that has fallen from the sky during a thunderstorm. Compose an autobiography of your life. Focus on your feelings as the matter in your body changed states. Describe a time when you were frozen into a solid and another instance when you were heated to evaporate into a gas. Where were you when these changes occurred? How did your atoms and molecules react to the changes in state? Discuss their movement. Include as many chemistry vocabulary words as possible in your story. *(Intrapersonal)*	Water is known as the universal solvent because it dissolves so many substances. A water molecule is polar. Research the difference between polar and non-polar molecules. Polar molecules will mix with each other and non-polar molecules will do the same. However, polar and non-polar molecules won't mix together. Using liquids or emulsions (such as mayonnaise) found around your home, discover 5 that will dissolve in water and 5 that won't. Display your results in a chart or demonstration for the class. What conclusions can you draw? *(Bodily/Kinesthetic, Verbal/Linguistic)*	Secure a bag of gumdrops that contains six different colors. Each gumdrop represents one atom. Assign a color to each of these elements: carbon, hydrogen, oxygen, chlorine, nitrogen, and sulfur. Using toothpicks as bonds, construct models of the following molecules: Carbon dioxide, water, nitrogen dioxide, sulfur dioxide and hydrochloric acid. Create a chart that identifies the chemical symbol for each molecule and the color associated with each element. *(Bodily/Kinesthetic, Visual/Spatial)*
Identify 8 common chemical compounds found in an average home. Using either their common names or their chemical formulas, create a rap naming them and explaining their importance to our lives. Perform the rap for your class. *(Musical/Rhythmic)*	Using a digital or video camera, take pictures of places and/or objects in the natural world where elements from the periodic table occur. Download your images onto a computer and create a slide show or movie, using a voice-over or labels to identify which elements are being illustrated. *(Naturalist)*	Choose a family of elements from the Periodic Table. Using your computer software, create a bar, circle, or line graph that compares/contrasts the number of protons, neutrons, and electrons found in each member element of the family. *(Mathematical/Logical)*

Think-Tac-Toe: Energy

Overview: These interactive projects provide students with the opportunity to review a wide variety of topics typically included in a study of energy. Students may work in small cooperative learning groups to develop and carry out the projects, or they may work to complete them independently. This is for the teacher to decide. Allowing students to choose the groupings, small group or independent, that they would prefer would add an additional element of learning profile differentiation to these tasks.

Standards: The student will:
- Analyze the various forms of energy, including light, heat, and sound
- Describe how these forms of energy behave as predictable phenomena in a variety of circumstances

Objectives:

The students will **KNOW**
- Key terms associated with a discussion of energy including convection, radiation, transfer, frequency, amplitude, conduction, expansion, and contraction.
- Key characteristics that describe the tenets of the Law of Conservation of Energy and Newton's Laws of Motion.

The students will **UNDERSTAND THAT**
- Heat flows through materials or across space from warm objects to cooler objects until both objects are at equilibrium.
- Sound demonstrates that vibrating materials generate waves that transfer energy.
- Light and matter physically interact with one another in predictable and observable ways.
- Energy (in any form) cannot be created or destroyed but can be changed from one form into another.

The students will **BE ABLE TO**
- Evaluate their current understandings of energy to discern and describe both qualitative and quantitative relationships associated with energy transfer and/or transformation.

Basis for Differentiation: Student learning profile (Gardner's Multiple Intelligences)

Science

Energy – The Task Options

Rube Goldberg Device *(logical-mathematical)*	**Chart Your Energy** *(naturalist)*	**Express Yourself** *(verbal-linguistic)*
Drawing on Newton's Laws *(visual-spatial)*	**Have your own idea? See your teacher to explain it and get it approved.**	**Sports Star** *(bodily-kinesthetic)*
Can You Hear Me Now? *(musical-rhythmic)*	**Feeling the Heat!** *(interpersonal)*	**Conserve Your Energy** *(intrapersonal)*

Rube Goldberg Device

A Rube Goldberg device is an elaborate set of interrelated machines that make up a larger system – all of which is designed to carry out a simple action, such as blowing out a candle or filling a glass with water (There is a great description of this at www.rube-goldberg.com.)

Your task is to design a Rube Goldberg device of your own! Figure out what sort of task it will accomplish. Make a detailed sketch of your device. Your drawing should also include a description of how, at each place, energy of one form is transferred to another as the device carries out your selected task.

Chart Your Energy

We have discussed in class a wide variety of forms of energy – heat, solar, nuclear, sound, chemical, electrical, and mechanical energy, to name a few.

Your job if you choose this assignment is to make a chart of all the different forms of energy you see utilized on a daily basis.

Choose a day to spend conscious effort observing the world around you. From the moment you wake until you go to bed that night, keep a list of all the places where you see examples of different types of energy at work (for example, as your dad starts the car in the morning, the combustion of gas in the engine is an example of chemical energy).

Be sure that your chart lists what kind of energy you observed as well as where and when you witnessed it.

Express Yourself

There are many common expressions in our everyday language that have, at the root of them, some reference to energy. Make a list of at least 10 common sayings, and beside each identify what "energy fact" this saying incorporates as its basis. For example, the saying "A rolling stone gathers no moss" discusses *energy in motion* or *kinetic energy* (as opposed to potential energy).

Drawing on Newton's Laws

Your task, if you decide to do this assignment, is to create a mural or a series of comic strips that illustrate Newton's Laws of Motion. They are as follows.
- The force of friction retards motion.
- For every action there is an equal and opposite reaction.
- The greater the force, the greater the change in motion.
- An object's motion is the result of the combined effect of all forces acting on the object.
- A moving object that is not subjected to a force will continue to move at a constant speed in a straight line.
- An object at rest will remain at rest.

Your mural or comic strip may be interpretive or symbolic, but it must refer to all of Newton's Laws in some clever way. If you are in doubt as to whether others will understand what your mural or comic strip is illustrating, submit a written piece that explains it.

Can You Hear Me Now?

Whether it is a woodwind or a guitar, all musical instruments illustrate one very important concept: vibrating materials generate waves that transfer energy. It is our ears that translate these vibrations into what we hear as sound.

Your task is to compose a song that explains this to your classmates. Your song should incorporate, correctly, the following words and ideas associated with our study of sound energy: *frequency, amplitude, loudness, a brief description of how sound behaves differently as it travels through different material,* and *a brief discussion of the form and function of the human ear.*

Bonus points if you demonstrate using a musical instrument!

Science

Conserve Your Energy

The Law of Conservation of Energy states, among other ideas, that energy cannot be created or destroyed, but only changed from one form into another.

Think of a process in which energy is transformed from one form to another several different times (such as when making and baking a cake). Now, pretend that you are a form of energy (solar, heat, chemical, potential, kinetic, etc.) in that process.

Create a journal that describes what it is like to be you as you undergo the various changes from one form to the next. Be sure to use correct scientific vocabulary as you describe the transformations of energy.

Sports Star

Think of a sport with which you are very familiar. Think of ways in which this sport could be used as a metaphor for describing the physical interactions of *light and matter,* specifically the following concepts: *absorption, scattering,* and *how color is perceived.* You may also include any references about how the form and function of the human eye aids in our ability to perceive light.

Example: In football, there are "special teams." The purpose of these teams is to specifically master and execute certain portions of a football game – for example, kicking-off or receiving. In this way, there are certain cells in the eyes, rods, and cones, whose functions are to interpret visual stimulus in specific ways. The rods create a coarse grey image, which is adequate for seeing in poor light. The cones, on the other hand, interpret color and fine detail.

Feeling the Heat

With a partner (or partners) your task is to analyze and explain to the class how heat affects materials that might be used in technological design.

To do this, you and your partner(s) should create a series of short (1-2 minutes each) skits that demonstrate in some visual and memorable way: (1) how heat is conducted through materials, and (2) how heat (or lack thereof) causes materials to expand and contract.

Use of props may be helpful in demonstrating these concepts to the rest of the class.

Complex Instruction: Ecology and the Chesapeake Bay

Overview: These Complex Instruction tasks enable students to work in mixed-ability, learning profile-based groups of four while examining the ecology of Virginia's Chesapeake Bay and working collaboratively to create a final product. Each task requires research that group members can do together. As this research is completed, students work on tasks of their choosing. In this way, students are required to work both cooperatively and independently as they answer different types of questions and complete different types of products.

Standards:
- Identify components of an ecosystem
- Describe how human activities modify soil, water, and air quality
- Evaluate data related to population growth
- Identify that change in environmental conditions can affect the survival of individuals and of species
- Analyze practices that affect the use, availability, and management of natural resources

Objectives:
The students will **KNOW**
- Geographical elements of the Chesapeake Bay.
- Natural resources (past and present) available in and around the Chesapeake Bay.
- Changes that have taken place over time in and around the Chesapeake Bay.

The students will **UNDERSTAND THAT**
- Human population growth impacts the environment in a variety of ways.
- Examining the impact we have on one place can help us understand our global impact.
- Past decisions impacted the environment we have inherited, and our present-day decisions will impact the environment of the future.
- Natural resources are often limited.
- Native Americans of the past had a very different relationship with the environment than many people have today.

The students will **BE ABLE TO**
- Conduct research.
- Compare and contrast the Chesapeake Bay of the past and the present.
- Analyze changes over time in the Chesapeake Bay.
- Synthesize information to solve a problem.
- Work cooperatively and independently.

Basis for Differentiation: Student learning profile (Gardner's Multiple Intelligences as well as the need to think divergently) with some flexibility to address readiness differences (for instance, the need for structure versus open-endedness, clearly defined problems versus less defined ones)

📄 Introduction to All Tasks

As you gaze out over the still waters of the Chesapeake Bay, the morning fog is rising above the calm surface. It is the second day of your school field trip to Virginia's coastal areas.

Your group's first activity of the day is a nature walk through a cypress swamp in First Landing State Park. As you leave the Bay's shore, your group meanders across the swamp lands. You spy a large mound of oyster shells away from the path. You leave your group, walk over to the pile of shells, bend over, and scoop up a handful.

Suddenly, you are enveloped in a swirling cloud of mist. Out of this mist steps what appears to be a Native American from your Social Studies textbook. This spirit says to you with tears in his eye, *"Our bay is dying. Will you help make it strong again? If you agree to help, then I, Chesepioc, will guide you."*

The tasks will help your group make decisions about how to help Chesepioc and the Chesapeake Bay.

After each of the tasks is completed (and you will have to help one another to successfully complete them all), as a group you will compose a letter to the governors of Virginia and Maryland. First, this letter will summarize what you have come to know and understand about the Bay through your research. Second, it will offer your group's suggestions for improving the health of the Bay.

You must include justification for each of your recommendations. Your ultimate goal with this letter is to persuade the governors to take action so that you can fulfill your promise to Chesepioc.

Task One: The Travel Agent (visual/spatial, mathematical/logical)

Your group's success requires some current background knowledge about the Chesapeake Bay. Your job is to research facts, and include them in a short travel guide about the Bay. Your guide, which will serve as a resource for people visiting the Bay areas, will include the following components:

Maps:
- A map showing the Bay as a part of the state of Virginia
- A map showing the entire Chesapeake Bay

Watershed:
- A detailed explanation of a watershed
- The size of the Chesapeake Bay's watershed

Statistics:
- How many people live in the Chesapeake Bay watershed?
- How may miles of shoreline does the Bay have?
- How long and wide is the Bay?
- How deep is the Bay?
- What makes the Bay an estuary?

Task Two: The Historian (verbal/linguistic)

Your group's success requires that you know something about the history of the Chesapeake Bay. Your job is to research its history to find out what it was like in the 1600s when Chesepioc's tribe roamed the area. Then you will create a tribal journal that is a true reflection of Chesepioc's memories of and feelings about the Bay of the 1600s. Write the journal from Chesepioc's point of view and as if he was dictating his memories to you. To create this journal, you must address the following questions:

- Who lived by the Chesapeake Bay?
- What kinds of wildlife made up the Bay's ecosystem, and what were the most abundant types of plant and animal life?
- How did the Native Americans use the resources of the Bay – the land, the water, and the wildlife – to survive?
- Did the use of the Bay by the Native Americans harm the Bay? If so, how? If not, why not?
- What was the quality of the water in the Bay as Chesepioc remembers it?
- How did the Native Americans travel in the area?

Science

Task Three: The Ecologist (mathematical/logical)

Your group's success requires that you have up-to-date information about the current condition of the Chesapeake Bay. This information will allow your group to examine how the Bay has changed over time and to identify steps that can be taken to save it. After researching current data about the Chesapeake Bay, you will create a chart (make sure it has a title!) that clearly shows the following:

- Who lives by the Bay?
- How do modern Americans use the resources – the land, the water, and the wild-life – of the Bay?
- What other uses do modern Americans make of the Bay?
- What data can be found that indicates harm is being done to the Bay?
- What kinds of wildlife make up the Chesapeake Bay's ecosystem?
- What is the quality of the water in the Bay today?

Task Four: The Philosopher/Thinker (the existential, creative thinker)

Your group's success requires, as solving problems often does, a creative approach. The following questions ask you to think out of the box. Use what you know about the Chesapeake Bay to respond to them, and then, for each question, compose a paragraph that explains your reasoning.

Which one of the following attributes would be most helpful in restoring the health of the Chesapeake Bay?
- The talents of Harry Potter and his friends at Hogwarts
- The strength of King Kong
- The courage and compassion of Pocahantas

Is the Chesapeake Bay more like a multi-layered box of chocolates or a bag of potato chips? Why?

Choose an animal that is most like you that lives in the Chesapeake Bay or in the surrounding area. Why is this animal like you? What conditions exist in the Bay today that either help or hinder your survival?

Algae is to the Chesapeake Bay as _____ is to the Blue Ridge Mountains. Explain your analogy. What is the relationship between algae and the Chesapeake Bay that causes you to complete it this way?

Complex Instruction: Weather/Storms

Overview: These complex instruction tasks invite students to examine in depth and create interesting and unusual products about storms – a topic that is generally of high interest to students. Students are grouped in heterogeneous groups of five to complete the tasks provided. A variety of resources providing information about storms, including the Internet, should be available as students work on their tasks.

Standards:
- Build an understanding of weather and climate
- Analyze weather systems

Objectives:
The students will **KNOW**
- Characteristics of different types of storms.
- Causes and effects of storms.
- Famous storms.
- Weather-related vocabulary.

The students will **UNDERSTAND THAT**
- Weather is a system made up of different parts.
- Storms are part of the weather system and are systems themselves.
- There is much that can be predicted about storms and much that cannot be predicted about them.
- Severe storms can have a significant impact on people, animals, and places.
- Though we cannot control storms, we can control how we respond to and prepare for them.

The students will **BE ABLE TO**
- Describe, compare, and contrast storms.
- Explain how storms develop and grow.
- Discuss the consequences of storms.

Basis for Differentiation: Student learning profile (Gardner's Multiple Intelligences)

📄 **Directions**　　Work in your group to complete each of the following tasks. The tasks each require different abilities and skills so you should spend some time deciding who will take the lead on each task. However, as a group, you are responsible for completing all of the tasks. Planning is crucial. Who will be the leader for each task? Who will work on each task? How will you help one another? It may be helpful to note which tasks seems to overlap a bit.

Your final products should be neat, accurate, detailed, and thoughtful, and they should demonstrate fully your understanding of storms.

Science

Task One *(the writer)*

You are a storm. Keep a detailed journal, including both pictures and words, of your "life" from beginning to end. What do you do? What happens to you? How do you change? How do you feel about it?

Task Two *(the philosopher)*

Can we and should we control nature? In answering this question, you must provide ample supporting evidence for your thinking and reasoning. Prepare a speech to respond to the question.

Task Three *(the artist)*

Research famous US storms. Create a map that shows their paths from start to finish. What patterns do you see? Create a colorful and clear way to show these patterns. What conclusions can you draw?

Task Four *(the historian)*

Pick two famous US storms to research in depth. What kinds of storms were they? What was their impact on the US? Why did they have these impacts? Create an original and creative way to show their similarities and differences.

Task Five *(the imagination)*

Create a storm. What kind of storm is it and what path does it follow? What are its defining characteristics and its effects on people and places? Be detailed and clear.

Chapter 7: Social Studies

Tiered Assignments: American Revolution

Overview: These tiered activities provide students with the opportunity to discover why the colonists chose to become Patriots or Loyalists during the American Revolution. Students work independently to complete tasks at their appropriate readiness levels. All students begin with the same scenario (presented as *"Where Will You Stand?"*) and then complete their assigned tasks.

Standards:
- Identify the issues of dissatisfaction that led to the American Revolution
- Identity how political ideas shaped the revolutionary movement in America
- Describe key events and the roles of key individuals in the American Revolution

Objectives:
The students will **KNOW**
- The main causes of the American Revolution.
- Key individuals important to the American Revolution.
- The positions held by Loyalists and Patriots leading up to and during the American Revolution.

The students will **UNDERSTAND THAT**
- The colonists disagreed over the need to break away from England.
- The American Revolution divided families.
- People make individual choices based upon their experiences and beliefs.
- Key figures in the American Revolution persuaded colonists to support one side or the other.

The students will **BE ABLE TO**
- Describe the impact that important figures had on the American Revolution.
- Compare and contrast competing arguments and viewpoints.
- Conduct research to make an informed choice.
- Make and defend a choice.

Basis for Differentiation: Student readiness with regard to:
- structure versus open-endedness
- concreteness versus abstractness
- need to work with real-world situations
- ability to think creatively

Tier One = lower readiness
Tier Two = middle readiness
Tier Three = higher readiness

Social Studies

📄 *WHERE WILL YOU STAND? An Introduction to the Assignments*

It is early in the year 1775 in Williamsburg, Virginia. Your family has been arguing angrily about the role that the Royalist British government has in the life of the American colonists. Tempers in your home and on both sides of the Atlantic are rising. Your father is a strong supporter of King George III and does not want the colonies to break away from England. Your oldest brother is angry and excited about the thoughts of colonial independence from the King. The Boston Tea Party has already stirred the waters toward revolution and caused the colonists to begin to take sides. Shots have been fired between the British soldiers and colonial Minutemen. War is coming! Where will you stand – with the Loyalists or the Patriots?

In order to complete your task, you will need to use your classroom and school resources (for example, texts, primary documents, websites, and reference materials), as well as lecture and discussion notes to research the causes of the American Revolution, the positions held by the Loyalists and Patriots, and important people who contributed to the efforts of both sides.

Tier One

Your task is to fully describe your father and your brother, remembering that your father is loyal to the King of England and that your brother is planning to join the Virginia militia to fight against the British. The descriptions of your father and brother must include the following information:

Name
Occupation
Religion
Birthplace
Education
Land owner status
Physical appearance and dress

Using the information gained from your research, you will
   1) Write two detailed, descriptive paragraphs – one for your father and one for your brother
   2) Create a visual or illustration representing each character
   3) Compose a short speech to be given by each character explaining his position in the fight against England

© **Pieces of Learning**

Tier Two

The *Virginia Gazette* has asked your father and brother to conduct interviews with important Revolutionary figures. To make the articles more interesting, the newspaper has requested that your father interview a Patriot and that your brother interview a Loyalist. First, you must research the following Revolutionary figures and determine where their loyalties lie.

Lord Dunsmore   George Mason   Patrick Henry   Marquette Lafayette

Sir Thomas Gage   Thomas Jefferson   Benedict Arnold   James Madison

Jack Jouett   Baron Von Steuben   Francis Scott Key   General Cornwallis

Next, select the individuals whom your father and brother will interview. Create eight to 10 questions that they will ask to learn more about the person's childhood, occupation, involvement in the Revolutionary War, and unique characteristics. Finally, prepare and write the interview in paragraph form to be published in the *Virginia Gazette*.

Social Studies

Tier Three

The actions of both your father and brother could be seen as either terrorist acts or patriotic acts, depending upon your point of view. The following questions ask you to think outside of the box as you examine the distinction between loyalty and terrorism both during the American Revolution and in present times.

Answer these questions in writing using *strong supporting details*.

1) Is the desire for independence more like a house cat or a cheetah? Why?

2) Which is hotter – the Quartering Act or the Stamp Act? Why?

3) Choose a phrase from the list below that you feel symbolizes taxation without representation, and explain how this phrase represents it for you. Compose a paragraph explaining your choice and your thinking.

> Broken bones
> Regular chores
> Forced bedtime
> Age restrictions on movies
> Computer filters
> Homework assignments

4) Would the Sons of Liberty be considered a terrorist group or a patriotic group? Why?

5) Where do you draw the line between acts of loyalty and acts of terrorism? When do acts of loyalty become terrorism? Your answer should include your definition of terrorism.

6) Is terrorism ever justified? Explain.

7) If your father or brother were involved in what you considered to be terrorists acts, what would you do and why?

Tiered Assignments: Ancient Egyptian Culture

Overview: These tiered activities provide students with the opportunity to review the reasons that the Nile River was such an important feature of Ancient Egypt's history and culture. Students work in small (3-4 students) groups to complete the assigned tasks at their appropriate learning levels. Students work on these assignments after completion of the unit or after a series of lessons about the Nile River's importance to Ancient Egyptian culture.

Standards:
- Locate Egypt in time and place
- Describe the development of social, political, and economic patterns in Ancient Egypt
- Explain the development of religious traditions in Ancient Egypt

Objectives:
The students will **KNOW**
- Key products and services the Nile provided Ancient Egyptians.
- Types of daily activities Ancient Egyptians engaged in that involved the use of the Nile.
- The unique advantages the Nile River's ecosystem offered to the development of the Ancient Egyptian civilization.

The students will **UNDERSTAND THAT**
- The Nile River's importance in the daily life of Ancient Egyptians affected their culture, shaped their history, and influenced their religion.
- Cultures are affected, even shaped, by their physical environment.
- The geography of an area, including (but not limited to) its ecosystems, weather patterns, and natural resources, affects the daily behaviors and economic activities of a culture or group of people.

The students will **BE ABLE TO**
- Describe the impact the Nile River had on the development of Ancient Egypt's civilization and culture.
- Brainstorm current understandings/knowledge of Ancient Egyptian history.
- Evaluate the relative importance of the Nile's unique qualities in the development of the Ancient Egyptian society.
- Synthesize understandings about the Nile River's particular role in Ancient Egypt in order to form generalizations about the importance of geography to any culture's development.

Basis for Differentiation: Student readiness with regard to:
- structure versus open-endedness
- concreteness versus abstractness
- level of thinking

**Tier One = lower readiness Tier Two = middle readiness
Tier Three = higher readiness**

Social Studies

Tier One

Using the *ABC Brainstorming* method, create a list that explains why settling on or near the Nile River was such an important part of Ancient Egypt's civilization. You may use single words or phrases. Be sure to consider the following in your discussion:

- Resources/products the Nile provided
- Services the Nile provided
- Daily activities associated with the Nile
- The different regional names associated with the Nile
- Plants and animals important to the Nile's ecosystem
- Famous pharaohs who used the Nile
- Religious symbols associated with the Nile

Be ready to share and defend your list as a review for the rest of the class.

In order to complete your task, you will need to use your classroom and school resources (for example, texts, websites, and reference materials), as well as lecture and discussion notes to review the material highlighted in this unit.

Tier Two

Create a series of analogies, modeled after the examples below, to explore the many important reasons why the Nile's environment was so critical to Ancient Egyptian culture. Be sure to thoroughly brainstorm the importance of the Nile to the Ancient Egyptian culture first, considering:

- Resources/products the Nile provided
- Services the Nile provided
- Daily activities associated with the Nile
- The different regional names associated with the Nile
- Plants and animals important to the Nile's ecosystem
- Famous pharaohs who used the Nile
- Religious symbols associated with the Nile

tree : paper : : (papyrus) : velum	Cupid : love : : (Hapi) : Nile

In order to complete your task, you will need to use your classroom and school resources (for example, texts, websites, and reference materials), as well as lecture and discussion notes to review the material highlighted in this unit.

© **Pieces of Learning**

Tier Three

Consider the following formula as a model for the assignment.

$$\textbf{Power during the Middle Ages} = \left[\frac{\textbf{land + heritage}}{\textbf{serfs}} \right]^{nobles}$$

"land" represents the number of acres a person of wealth might own

"serfs" represents the number of serfs living on that land available to work/farm it

"heritage" represents the number of years the family has owned that land

"nobles" represents the number of other noblemen ready to help defend the land

Create a mathematical formula, like the one above, to express the importance of the Nile as a central and key element to Ancient Egypt's civilization. The formula should:

- Include enough elements to show that you have really considered and brainstormed a wide variety of elements in this problem.
- Combine operations and groups of operations to show that your group has actually thought about the interaction of the formula's elements (rather than just throwing them all together with a few math symbols sprinkled in).
- Cleverly manipulate ideas. Will you group them? Separate them? Are there any large ideas that need to be sub-defined?
- Cleverly manipulate the mathematical operations. Multiplication or division? Addition or subtraction? Raising an idea to the power of another idea? How might these combinations of concepts affect one another?

To show that you understand the formula, each group member must be ready to explain the formula to the rest of the class.

In order to complete your task, you will need to use your classroom and school resources (for example, texts, websites, and reference materials), as well as lecture and discussion notes to review the material highlighted in this unit.

Tiered Assignments: Ancient Rome

Overview: These tiered, small-group activities provide students with the opportunity to investigate or review a wide variety of topics typically included in a study of Ancient Rome. Students work in groups to discuss the given questions at their appropriate learning level. It is assumed that these questions will be posed on different occasions – that is, each set of questions (religion, fall of the empire, emperors, and architecture) will be addressed as separate lessons. They are merely combined on these pages because they all relate to the study of Ancient Rome. Thus, after each group has worked on a given activity, all of the groups will share both the questions they worked to complete as well as the answers they formulated. Finally, some of these questions might best be posed after a lesson has been taught about the given topic. This is for teacher to decide.

Standards:
- Describe Roman mythology and religion
- Explain the social structure and role of slavery, significance of citizenship, and the development of democratic features in the government of the Roman Republic
- Assess the impact of military conquests on the army, economy, and social structure of Rome
- Assess the roles of a variety of emperors in the collapse of the Republic and the rise of imperial monarchs
- List contributions in art and architecture, technology and science, medicine, literature, history, language, religious institutions, and laws
- Cite the reasons for the decline and fall of the Roman Empire

Objectives:
The students will **KNOW**
- Key gods and goddesses that represent the concerns of Roman citizens.
- Types of architecture for which Rome is known and responsible for creating.
- Key emperors of the Roman Empire and their selected accomplishments.
- Key reasons why the Roman Empire eventually collapsed.

The students will **UNDERSTAND THAT**
- Ancient religions often served as a cathartic target to which Romans could release their worries in a time when science was not fully developed to explain natural phenomena.
- Cultural needs affect a culture's architecture, and architecture reflects the culture that uses it.
- Leaders of culture are often known, remembered, and even evaluated for more than what they accomplish as a political leader.
- The demise of social, cultural, economic, and political institutions are intertwined.

The students will **BE ABLE TO**
- Describe the impact that Ancient Rome's gods and goddesses had on the daily life of citizens.
- Discuss current understandings/knowledge of Ancient Roman history.
- Compare current cultural phenomena to key, identified areas of Ancient Rome's culture.

Basis for Differentiation: Student readiness with regard to:
- Structure versus open-endedness
- Concreteness versus abstractness
- Level of thinking based on Bloom's Taxonomy

Note to the teacher: It is assumed that as the students work to complete these discussion questions groups are unaware of the other groups' questions. The questions should not be revealed until it is time for groups to share responses. Furthermore, some questions require lists for the students to consult. The teacher should supply these lists using material that has been taught throughout implementation of his/her own unit design. Since no two teachers will cover the exact same lesson points in a broad survey of Ancient Rome, these lists have not been provided.

Tier One = lower readiness
Tier Two = middle readiness
Tier Three = higher readiness

Tier One Discussion Questions

Religion

Given a list of Roman gods, identify what role each god assumed as he/she affected the daily life of the Roman citizens (For example: Mars is the god of War.). Then choose three gods, and create a simple hand sign or gesture that could be used to represent what the chosen gods' duties were. Be ready to share this with the rest of the class.

Fall of the Empire

The Roman Empire fell apart for a variety of interconnected reasons. Make a list of causes that brought down the Empire. You should find at least five good reasons why Rome fell. Then, as a group, decide which factor played the most significant part in the fall of the Roman Empire, and be able to explain why you feel it is the most important.

Emperors

Given a list of Roman emperors, create a T-chart with their names in the left column and any significant events associated with their reigns listed in the right column. Then create a mnemonic device to share with the rest of the class to assist them in remembering these names and the key accomplishments of these Roman leaders. Caligula, Commodus, and Nero are among the more infamous of Rome's emperor's. Name modern-day leaders who are infamous, and detail why they are.

Architecture

Examine a given assortment of pictures showing Roman buildings, roads, aqueducts, etc. Sort them into three piles of your choice, being sure to label each pile with a unique, identifiable label. You may sort them according to looks, uses, etc. Then, using the pictures as a starting point, define, in your own words, *architecture*. Be ready to share this definition with your classmates.

Tier Two Discussion Questions

Religion

The Romans believed that their gods assumed human form and interacted with people on earth. Many of their myths were focused on this mingling of humans and gods. Choose one god, and discuss what story line could be created around that god visiting the earth in the present. Could one of the Roman myths surrounding this god be rewritten for modern times? How?

Fall of the Empire

The following are some of the reasons why the Roman Empire eventually collapsed.

- economic decay through looting of the treasury (by unscrupulous emperors and barbarians) and trade deficits
- barbarian invasions on many of Rome's borders
- decay of military strength due to attrition, disorganization, lack of leadership, and overzealous generals who sought power for themselves

Consider the list above, and then add to it any other reasons you can think of. Rank the reasons in order of importance, with #1 being the factor *most* contributing to the fall, and the last item on your list being the one that had, in your opinion, the *least* impact on Rome's fall. Be ready to justify your rankings.

Emperors

Caligula, Commodus, and Nero are among the more infamous of Rome's emperors; they are known more for their personal antics than for their ability to effectively lead the Roman Empire. Identify an example of a modern-day person who is more known for his/her *personality* than his *talents* in a particular area. Consider politicians, celebrities, etc. Be ready to justify your answer with details.

Architecture

The Pantheon, the Colloseum, and Hadrian's Wall are, among others, some of the most famous pieces of architecture from Ancient Rome. Create a list of other famous examples of architecture known around the world (for example, Paris' Eiffel Tower and Egypt's Pyramids). Then, using this list as a springboard, identify what these might have in common (if anything) in order to answer the following question for the class: *What does it take for a piece of architecture to be famous?* Be ready to share your list with the class so they can understand your point of reference.

Social Studies

Tier Three Discussion Questions

Religion

Ancient Romans often honored gods for natural phenomena that they did not understand, could not readily explain, or were afraid of. For example, Verminus was considered the god of the cattle worm, or simply disease. Consider today's world. What sorts of unusual phenomena occur today that seemingly have little explanation or that make us nervous? Make a list of these occurrences, and then, in the spirit of the ancient Romans, create a name for a god that might be called upon for aid. For example, Computerius might be the name of the god of computer crashes.

Fall of the Empire

The following are some of the reasons why the Roman Empire eventually collapsed.
- economic decay through looting of the treasury (by unscrupulous emperors and barbarians) and trade deficits
- barbarian invasions on many of Rome's borders
- decay of military strength due to attrition, disorganization, lack of leadership, and overzealous generals who sought power for themselves

Considering the list above in more general terms, think of a modern-day example of a "fall." You may consider individual people, other modern political regimes, or even companies or corporations (like Enron). Be sure to identify the reasons why your selection is an example of a "fall," and describe those factors that led to its decline.

Emperors

Rome began as a representative democracy and morphed into an empire where the emperor had absolute and complete control. The United States is also a representative democracy. How would our lives change today if:
- our government began invading other countries to bring them under our control to form an American Empire?
- one individual could usurp the power of all three branches of government and assume the role of an American Emperor, with all the powers given to an ancient Roman emperor?

During your discussion, be specific in identifying areas of our lives that would evidence change if the above two scenarios occurred, and describe what changes would take place.

Architecture

The architecture of a society reflects its values and the areas of life on which it places the most importance. After examining well-known examples of Roman architecture, discuss what these structures tell us about Roman values and the areas of Roman life that seemed to hold great importance for that society. When sharing the results with the class, be sure to distinguish which pieces of architecture led you to draw parallels between Roman values and important areas of Roman life.

© Pieces of Learning

Tiered Projects: Regions of the United States

Overview: These projects give students a chance to explore in depth the relationship between location and regional characteristics while working at appropriate levels of challenge. Students work in small, teacher-assigned groups that are based on students' interests. Some tasks within each tier are required while others offer students choices.

Standards:
- Describe the absolute and relative location of major landforms, bodies of water, and natural resources in the U.S.
- Analyze the impact of absolute and relative location of places on ways of living in the U.S.
- Define region and identify various regions within the U.S.

Objectives:
The students will **KNOW**
- Names of landforms and bodies of water.
- The regions of the U.S.
- Latitude and longitude and map symbols.

The students will **UNDERSTAND THAT**
- Location impacts the characteristics, such as climate, vegetation, and natural resources of a place or region.
- People choose where to live based on regional characteristics.

The students will **BE ABLE TO**
- Describe regional characteristics.
- Identify and locate landforms and bodies of water.
- Read and create maps.

Basis for Differentiation: Student readiness with regard to:
- knowledge of U.S. geography
- structure versus open-endedness
- ability to transfer information to create something new.

Student interest as students working at the lower tier choose which region to explore. Student learning profile as students at both tiers make choices about tasks that are based on *Multiple Intelligences*.

Tier One = lower readiness
Note to the teacher: The teacher will need to provide a graphic organizer to the students working on Tier One in order form them to complete their second task.

Tier Two = higher readiness
Note to the teacher: Students in this group take an assessment of their knowledge of the regions in the U.S. after reading information provided in their textbook.

Social Studies

Tier One: Explore-a-Region

1) From the list below, rank order the regions of the United States according to your interest in studying them (you will be assigned to a small group based on your preferences):

   - Northeast
   - Southeast
   - Middle West
   - Southwest
   - West
   - Alaska
   - Hawaii

2) Research information about your region using your textbook and the additional resources provided in the classroom and school media center. Then, complete the graphic organizer provided.

3) Create an original map that illustrates the landforms and bodies of water of your region. The map may be constructed out of a material of your choosing, but it must be geographically accurate. Be sure to provide a map key.

4) Complete one the of the following:
   - Create a poster that tells something interesting or unusual about your region. Be sure to include both words and pictures.
   - Create a travel brochure that would make someone want to visit your region.
   - Write an obituary about a famous person who lived and died in your region. What did he or she accomplish in his or her lifetime? Why is this person famous?
   - Write a newspaper article about an important event that occurred or occurs in your region. This event can be something historic (for example, a battle or a trial) or something that your region is known for (for example, a sporting event or a festival).

5) Would you want to live in this region? Why?

Tier Two: Create-a-Country

Create the boundaries of your country, and show its size to scale on a map that also shows its physical features. Your country must include at least six different landforms and four bodies of water. One of your country's landforms must be a mountain or a mountain range.

1) Show your country's absolute location using latitude and longitude and its relative location using already existing continents and countries.

2) Create a way to illustrate the climate regions and vegetation of your country.

3) Determine your country's natural resources, and explain how they are used to benefit the people living there.

4) Complete two of the following:
   - What kinds of animals are indigenous to your country? Your animal life must be compatible with the climate and vegetation available. You must also consider the food chain.
   - Select a location for the capital of your country, and explain why it is a suitable site for a large city that is the seat of your country's government.
   - Create a short history for your country. Who discovered it? Who settled it? How has it changed over time? Which countries are its enemies and allies? Explain why.
   - Create a national anthem for your country that reflects its history and people. You may write an original tune, or use an existing tune for which you change the words.
   - Create a dictionary of 15 to 20 words that are particular to people living in your country. For example, in England an elevator is called a *lift* and a bathroom is called a *loo*. What might they be called in your country?

RAFT: American Civil War

Overview: These RAFT assignments give students an opportunity to apply their knowledge of individuals important to the Civil War effort. This approach can be utilized with other important figures as well.

Standard:
- Evaluate the importance of the roles played by individuals leading up to and during the Civil War

Objectives:

The students will **KNOW**
- Key figures who made important contributions during the Civil War era.

The students will **UNDERSTAND THAT**
- People's actions can be influenced by the significant events occurring around them.
- The accomplishments of historical figures can inspire people to affect change in today's world.
- Historical figures can serve as role models for individuals who work in similar occupations today.

The students will **BE ABLE TO**
- Identify famous individuals who impacted the culture of the times and the war's progress.
- Conduct research.
- Relate past accomplishments to today's society.

Basis for Differentiation: Student interest with regard to significant individuals and their importance during the Civil War era

American Civil War

ROLE	AUDIENCE	FORMAT	TOPIC
An army surgeon operating on Civil War battlefields	People of the Union and the Confederacy	Letter published in a newspaper	Why I named Clara Barton the "Angel of the Battlefield"
Robert Todd Lincoln	Abraham Lincoln	A handmade card	Why I'm proud of my father
Traveller, Robert E. Lee's horse	Other horses in a stable at Appomattox	Speech	Why my master is the best of all generals in this Civil War
A literary critic	The general public living in the 1850s	A magazine article	Why Harriet Beecher Stowe's *Uncle Tom's Cabin* Will Still be Remembered 100 Years in the Future

RAFT: Geography of Latin America

Overview: These RAFT assignments give students an opportunity to apply their knowledge of the geography of Latin America (though this approach can be used with any geographic region). They are listed in order of difficulty with the first being the most difficult.

Standards:
- Identify key physical characteristics such as landforms, water forms, and climate regions
- Identify ways in which people have used, altered, and adapted to their environments in order to meet their needs
- Create maps, charts, graphs, databases, and models as tools to illustrate information about different people, places, and regions

Objectives:
The students will **KNOW**
- The main physical features of Latin America.
- The climate and vegetation of Latin America.
- Map skills.
- Vocabulary: plateau, pampas, isthmus, coral, tributary, El Niño, elevation.

The students will **UNDERSTAND THAT**
- Geography influences the way people live.
- Climate and vegetation affect how and where people live.
- There are many different climate regions in Latin America.

The students will **BE ABLE TO**
- Identify the physical features of a region.
- Describe, compare, and contrast geographic regions, climates, and vegetation.
- Use appropriate vocabulary related to geography.

Basis for Differentiation: Student readiness with regard to:
- knowledge of Latin American geography
- general thinking skills

Geography of Latin America

ROLE	AUDIENCE	FORMAT	TOPIC
The Aztecs	Present-day Latin Americans	Position paper	Humans can and should change the geography to meet their needs
Citizen of Latin America	People around the world	Speech	How my life is impacted by geography, climate, and vegetation
Student	Classmates	Three-column chart	How the physical geography and daily life of Latin America compare to where I live

Think-Tac-Toe: American Civil War

Overview: These Think-Tac-Toe options allow students to choose their own ways of showing what they have come to know and understand about the causes, events, and consequences of the American Civil War. The tasks are structured according to Gardner's Theory of Multiple Intelligences, with each of the eight intelligences being represented. Students may choose any three options going across, down, or diagonally within the grid. This Think-Tac-Toe is to be utilized as one of the culminating activities for a unit on the Civil War and can be combined with other formal assessments to evaluate student learning.

Standards:
- Analyze American attempts to abolish slavery and how the issues of states' rights and slavery increased sectional tensions
- Examine and analyze the multiple causes, key events, and effects of the American Civil War
- Evaluate the importance of the roles played by individuals during the Civil War

Objectives:
The students will **KNOW**
- Cultural, economic, and cultural issues that divided the nation.
- Key figures who played important roles in events leading to and during the war.
- Critical events in the war including major battles.
- The effects of war on Union and Confederate soldiers.

The students will **UNDERSTAND THAT**
- Slavery was an institution that prohibited the ideals of the Declaration of Independence from being realized.
- A civil war divides all aspects of a society and negatively impacts individuals regardless of their socio-economic level.
- The American Civil War had significant social and economic impacts on the nation.

The students will **BE ABLE TO**
- Conduct research.
- Describe the daily life of a Civil War soldier.
- Compare and contrast life in the mid-1800s to the present.
- Make inferences.
- Justify thinking and defend choices.
- Define one's own interpretation of the impact of slavery on 19th century American life.
- Identify famous individuals who impacted the culture of the times and the war's progress.

Basis for Differentiation: Student learning profile (Gardner's Multiple Intelligences)

Think-Tac-Toe: American Civil War

Create a dictionary of words and phrases which were commonly used by either Union or Confederate soldiers during the Civil War. When researching these terms, consider weaponry, everyday items carried by soldiers, military commands, food, clothing, survival, etc. *(Verbal/Linguistic)*	You are a Southern landowner whose home has been secured as a military hospital. Research medical procedures practiced during the Civil War. Create a visual representation – a poster, mural, collage, etc. – that illustrates how medicine was practiced in the war field. You may use words as labels, if desired. Your visuals may be hand-drawn, computer generated, or taken from the Internet. *(Visual/Spatial)*	Identify two famous abolitionists. Investigate their lives to discover what actions they took to try to eliminate slavery in the United States. Compose a dialogue between the two abolitionists in which they discuss how they chose to bring about change in attitudes, how successful they were in achieving their goals, and how their approaches to removing slavery from our society compared and contrasted. *(Interpersonal)*
You will assume the role of a newspaper editor in either the state of New York or the state of Virginia. Compose an editorial for your newspaper that expresses your opinion of the institution of slavery as it existed in America in the years right before the Civil War. Provide examples from your research to justify your opinions. *(Intrapersonal)*	Create an ABC book on important individuals and events relating to the Civil War. Each page of the book should include a unique display of the alphabet letter in the format, "A is for ____". After deciding upon the person or event to place in the blank, compose a short description of the importance of your choice to the Civil War. Include an appropriate illustration on each page: hand-drawn or computer-generated. *(Visual/Spatial, Verbal/Linguistic)*	Choose an important battle that occurred during the Civil War. Research the military strategies and other issues that impacted the outcome of the battle. Design a board game that will lead the players through the battle, and help them understand the successes and failures of each side, as well as the impact of the battle on the war. Play the game with your classmates. *(Bodily/Kinesthetic)*
Choose an important Union or Confederate general or an important government figure such as President Lincoln. Compose a song celebrating his contributions to the war effort that both soldiers and civilians will enjoy singing. You may set your words to an existing tune or compose a melody of your own. *(Musical/Rhythmic)*	A young soldier has just been recruited into your unit. Your job is to explain to him the importance of the natural environment in the success of military combat. Research the roles that landforms, bodies of water, weather, and disease played in Civil War battles. Compose a short manual that will help this new soldier understand how natural elements will affect the war. *(Naturalist)*	Choose any aspect of the Civil War that interests you and that generates data you can research. Construct a graph (line, bar, or circle) that illustrates your findings. Examples of topics would include: the number of battles fought in each state, numbers of soldiers who fought from each state or who were killed from each state, the numbers of deaths in major battles, etc. *(Math/Logical)*

Think-Tac-Toe: U.S. Government

Overview: These Think-Tac-Toe options allow students to choose their own ways of showing what they have come to know and understand about some fundamental principles set forth in the U.S. Constitution. Students must choose an option from each row. Thus, all students will complete three products that address the branches of U.S. government (first row), the system of checks and balances (second row), and the process for amending the U.S. Constitution (third row). The work the students complete can be combined with more formal assessment to evaluate what students have learned over the course of a unit or series of lessons on U.S. government.

Standards:
- Analyze how the U.S. Constitution reflects the principles of checks and balances and separation of powers
- Summarize the purposes for and processes of changing the U.S. Constitution

Objectives:
The students will **KNOW**
- The branches of government and their powers.
- Examples of checks and balances among the branches of government.
- Constitutional amendments and the process required for amending the U.S. Constitution.

The students will **UNDERSTAND THAT**
- The U.S. Constitution defines how our federal government works.
- The U.S. Constitution defines the three branches of government and their roles and divides power among them so that no one branch becomes too strong.
- The process of amending the Constitution reflects federalism and the power of the people.
- Amendments to the Constitution allow people to respond to current issues and questions.

The students will **BE ABLE TO**
- Describe, compare, and contrast the powers of the executive, legislative, and judicial branches of government.
- Explain and justify the U.S. government's system of checks and balances.
- Analyze the process of amending the U.S. Constitution.

Basis for Differentiation: Student learning profile (Gardner's Multiple Intelligences)

Think-Tac-Toe: U.S. Government

If you could choose, which branch of government would you most like to be a member of? Why? Justify your choice in a paragraph. Be sure to address the specific powers and responsibilities that you would have in that branch and how they would differ from those of another branch. *(Verbal, Intrapersonal)*	Write a conversation between two members of different branches of government in which each person discusses his or her roles and responsibilities in government. How will these people describe themselves and their work? How will they compare what they do as members of government? *(Verbal, Interpersonal)*	Create a new symbol for each of the branches of government. Each of the symbols should fully demonstrate the role of each branch as well as its specific powers. Then create a short, written statement explaining each of your original symbols. *(Visual, Verbal)*
Create a visual, using both pictures and words, that clearly shows how the U.S. government's system of checks and balances works. Your work should help younger viewers to better understand the relationships among the three branches of government. Be sure to explain why checks and balances are needed. *(Visual, Verbal)*	How does a system of checks and balances work in nature? Find a way to show how this system in nature compares to this system in the U.S. government. What would happen if both nature and the U.S. government did not have this type of system? Use both words and pictures to support your thinking. *(Naturalist, Visual, Verbal)*	Research the philosophy of Baron de Montesquieau. How did his thinking influence the authors of the U.S. Constitution? Write a paragraph explaining what you find. Write a second paragraph providing your opinion of his philosophy. *(Verbal, Researcher, Philosopher)*
You are a recently ratified amendment to the U.S. Constitution. Create a visual map that illustrates your journey to ratification. Where did you begin? How did you get to the end of your journey? What "difficulties" did you come up against on your journey to ratification? *(Visual)*	Select an event, question, or problem that led to an amendment to the Constitution. How did this amendment respond to a particular issue? What might be different about our society today if this amendment had not been ratified? Write a paragraph summarizing your findings and opinions. *(Verbal)*	You are serving on a committee whose mission is to choose which amendment to the Constitution ratified during the 1900s has had the biggest effect on American society. Which amendment will receive your vote and why? Prepare a short speech to be delivered to the rest of your committee. *(Verbal, Kinesthetic)*

Complex Instruction: Philosophers of Ancient Greece

Overview: These complex instruction tasks invite students to work creatively while examining the different philosophies of Socrates, Aristotle, and Plato. Students work in small groups of three and may need to use classroom and school resources as well as the Internet to expand on their textbook readings about these philosophers. Following the completion of these tasks, students can engage in small or whole group discussions about the influence of past thinkers on the way we live and think today and can begin to evaluate their own philosophies.

Standards:
- Recognize and analyze the achievements of Ancient Greek civilization
- Assess the enduring contributions of the Ancient Greeks

Objectives:
The students will **KNOW**
- The fundamental philosophies of Socrates, Aristotle, and Plato.

The students will **UNDERSTAND THAT**
- Philosophers and thinkers through time have been affected by and have reflected the times and cultures in which they have lived.
- Thinkers of the past have impacted ideas in the present.
- Examining different philosophies invites us to examine our own as well.

The students will **BE ABLE TO**
- Explain, compare, and contrast the philosophies of Socrates, Aristotle, and Plato.
- Conduct research.
- Connect the past and the present.

Basis for Differentiation: Student learning profile

Task One (the artist)

Create three cartoon strips of at least three frames each that demonstrate the philosophies of Socrates, Aristotle, and Plato (one cartoon strip will address Socrates, another will address Aristotle, and the last will address Plato). You must address these philosophers' ideas about leadership/government and its role in the lives of people, education, and ethics. What scenarios might you be able to use to illustrate their ideas?

Lastly, create another cartoon of at least three frames that shows how their philosophies are at work in today's society.

Task Two (the writer)

Create the dialogue for a panel discussion that you facilitate that includes Socrates, Aristotle, and Plato. This panel discussion should help us get to know each of these philosophers and his ideas. Be sure to have them answer questions that give us insight into their thoughts about leadership/government and its role in the lives of people, education, and ethics. How might they respond to one another's ideas? Let them do the talking!

Then write a paragraph explaining how these ancient philosophers' ideas are at work in today's society.

Task Three (the performer)

Write and perform a one-person show in which you play these three ancient Greek philosophers: Socrates, Aristotle, and Plato. If they could talk to us now, what might they say about their ideas about leadership/government and its role in the lives of people, education, and ethics? How might they state their philosophies?

Your performance should be both entertaining and informative. Be sure to end it by explaining how these philosophers' ideas are still relevant today.

Complex Instruction: The Middle Ages

Overview: These complex instruction tasks expand on the study of the Middle Ages in Europe and allow students to explore more deeply specific aspects of medieval culture and society. Students work in small groups of four. Individuals within each group select and complete a task to be worked on independently, and group members may collaborate and assist one another as needed to ensure completion of all of the tasks. Resources for research should be provided in the classroom.

Standards:
- Describe and analyze changes that have occurred in ways of living in Europe
- Identify people, symbols, and events associated with the heritage of societies of Europe
- Trace an economic, political, or social development through the history of Europe

Objectives:
The students will **KNOW**
- Famous events and people of the Middle Ages.
- Social and political structures of the Middle Ages.

The students will **UNDERSTAND THAT**
- Culture is defined by how people live, the language they use, the belief systems they have, and change.
- Understanding the past gives us insight into the present.
- Throughout time, people and events have impacted the course of history.

The students will **BE ABLE TO**
- Compare and contrast the past and the present.
- Make connections.
- Draw conclusions.
- Work independently and cooperatively.
- Conduct research to answer questions.

Basis for Differentiation: Student learning profile (Gardner's Multiple Intelligences) and interest with regard to various aspects of the Middle Ages

Task One (mathematical/logical learner)

The Black Death had a major impact on medieval society. Research this medical nightmare using the resources provided.

First, list the causes and symptoms of the plague.

Second, create a graph that shows how it affected the population of Europe. Make sure that you label your graph so that viewers can see clearly the impact the Black Death had on the population.

Then create a second graph showing how a modern-day plague has impacted or is impacting a part of our world today.

How is our modern-day plague similar to the Black Death?

Task Two (verbal/linguistic and interpersonal learner)

Feudalism defined medieval society and an individual's place in it.

Create a dialogue between a lord, a serf, and a knight that demonstrates each person's opinion and feelings about feudalism. Make sure that each person backs up his opinion with evidence.

Then compose a speech that tells your thoughts about feudalism. Was it a good system? Why or why not? Would it work today? Why or why not?

Social Studies

Task Three (verbal/linguistic and mathematical/logical learner)

Research Old English.

Create a graphic organizer that shows how at least 20 words in modern English are derived from Old English. It may help to include words from Middle English as well.

Show that some words have changed more than others through the ages.

Can you draw any conclusions about the differences between the words that have not changed very much and the words that have changed a great deal? Why have some words changed more than others?

- -

Task Four (visual/spatial learner)

You are a cartoonist who has a flair for poking fun at people and their quirky customs and behaviors.

Create a series of at least six one-frame cartoons that points out some of the more interesting (or odd) aspects of medieval society. You must address different aspects of medieval life in each cartoon.

What might a humorist have to say about feudalism? Primogeniture? Knighthood? The crusades? How about medieval monastery life?

Make sure that your cartoons are based on fact!

Chapter 8: Assessing Learning in a Differentiated Classroom

Not everything that can be counted counts,
and not everything that counts can be counted.

Albert Einstein

Several years ago, one of us attended a presentation titled "Differentiation and Assessment" at a national conference. The large presentation room was packed with teachers, parents, consultants, researchers, and university faculty from all around the country. There was also one very nervous graduate student. On her way into the room, this graduate student, who was also the presenter, uttered, *"I really don't know what to say about this."*

As it turned out, she really did not have to say much. She showed two overheads on the screen. One announced the title of the presentation, and the other offered equally little: a simple quote about grading. Within two minutes, the audience erupted. The attendees expressed a wide array of concerns about grades and testing. They described instances in which students had been treated unfairly in the assessment proc-

ess. They pointed out how seemingly impossible it is to create rubrics, which themselves had to be differentiated. They worried about how difficult it is to remove the subjective aspects of grading from what, at least in theory, should be largely objective in nature.

The members of the audience raised some important issues. And no consensus was reached. At the end of the hour, they left the room feeling just as frustrated and confused as when they had entered, and the graduate student was left holding the remainder of her overheads and wondering where the time had gone.

Assessment is a "sticky wicket" whether we differentiate or not. And there are no easy answers to the problems it presents. This is especially true as high-stakes, state testing becomes more and more the focus of school districts across the country and impacts our work

Assessment

in our classrooms and in our schools. That being said, we do believe that there are ways to make assessment more effective and efficient, even within the complex process of differentiation.

When we work with teachers and the topic of grading crops up (and it *always* does), we begin the discussion by asking everyone to consider the purposes of grades. *Why do we have them? What are they supposed to do?*

The answers to these questions are always the same: *"They communicate information to students, parents, and teachers about how a student is doing in a particular subject." "They tell us what the students 'got' during a unit of study." "Grades let us as teachers know how well we've taught the material in a unit of study."* Indeed these are valid ways of thinking about the role of grades.

But we would like to add to these ideas that grades also provide us with an opportunity to see what students are still missing. Herein lies the primary difference between assessment in a traditional classroom environment and assessment in a differentiated one: In the former, it

serves as an ending, like the close of a chapter in that portion of study during the school year. In a differentiated learning environment, it is both an ending point and a beginning point.

Assessment in a differentiated classroom must be ongoing and flexible. It should serve as the foundation for instructional decision making. As stated in Chapter 1, the cycle of assessment and instruction in a differentiated classroom ensures that each student is offered opportunity for both challenge and success with the tasks she is given. It is not simply the "event" that occurs at the end of each unit or marking period.

This is, of course, a tall order. But it does not mean that we have to throw out our grade books. It means, instead, that we must adjust or modify both the ways we *collect* data about our students and the ways we *use* that data to plan our instruction. To this end, here we offer some tips for getting the most out of classroom assessment.

1) **Pre-assess wisely**. Often teachers give a unit pre-assessment and then fail to use what they learn from it. The temptation to ignore the results of a pre-assessment is strong. We as teachers – constantly squeezed by the pressures of grading, designing lessons, communicating with parents, and a host of other teaching responsibilities – might feel that reviewing pre-assessments is just another time-consuming task we must do. It is one that is easy to skip. Don't! We advise giving yourself time to use what you learn by giving a pre-assessment one to two weeks before a unit begins. This gives you ample time to check the pre-assessments and analyze the results. Are there some items that all or no students missed? Or are there items on which there are a wide range of responses? Did the results of the pre-assessment indicate to you that there are portions of the upcoming unit where everyone seems weak? Conversely, did the results show you areas of strength for the group as a whole? Knowing the answers to questions such as these will help you plan your unit accordingly. The time is takes to go through this process might very well be saved in skipping material that the bulk of your students already know.

2) **Never reinvent the wheel**. This one's simple: If your curriculum resources provide assessments, use them as pre-assessments. A unit post-test for that math or language arts textbook chapter can easily serve as your pre-assessment, and it can be used again at the end of the unit along with other forms of assessment. Similarly, ask fellow teachers for samples of quizzes and tests they have created over the years. Share and share alike. Many schools have created department file cabinets or places where teachers of a common subject area can place copies of materials and assessments they use.

3) **Assess frequently and quickly**. There are certainly times in our instruction when a lengthy, deep assessment is needed, and students need to learn how to prepare for and take these types of assessments. However, there are other times when a "short and sweet" assessment can be highly effective. Because assessment

drives instruction in a differentiated classroom and because teachers generally do not have a lot of extra time for additional grading, we suggest that you consider assessing frequently but that you also keep most of your assessment tools fairly short and focused. Short "checkpoints" throughout a unit help to ensure that students are progressing and meeting the necessary objectives along the way. The "3-2-1" strategy is a great one for quickly finding out what students have grasped during a lesson or activity. A social studies teacher might ask students to do the following on index cards a few minutes before leaving class:

3: Describe 3 powers of the legislative branch of government

2: Explain 2 ways that the legislative branch's power is limited

1: Write 1 question you still have about the legislative branch

A quick review of the index cards should give the teacher a good idea of what the students understand and what they need more work with about the legislative branch.

4) **Vary assessment formats**. Allowing students to show what they know, understand, and can do in a variety of different ways over the course of a unit gives them the opportunity to practice different skills while showing what they have learned. The reality, of course, is that many of our students will have to take the state-mandated test near the end of the year, and it is a multiple choice one. So, of course, they should be asked to complete some multiple choice assessments along the way. This is, after all, the best and *only* way they can learn the strategies needed for taking them successfully. However, multiple choice tests should be mixed with other formats, including more informal assessments such as journals and graphic organizers. Keep in mind that, in the end, we as teachers are interested in knowing how well students know and understand the material so that we can use that information in our own planning. If the students do not grasp the material initially, they will never be successful when asked to take that standardized state assessment in May. To this end, give students a wide variety of ways to

show you what they know. Consider some alternate (and equally informative) forms of assessment.

"In the Box" Assessments	*"Out of the Box" Assessments*
Tests	Cartoons
Quizzes	Interviews/conversations
Worksheets	Graphic organizers
Book reports	Journal entries
Essays	Maps
Homework	Musical collage
Short answer questions	Computer discussion boards

Opportunities for assessment abound. What this really means is that we ought to consider almost everything that happens in a classroom potentially useful as assessment data. What do students say during small- and whole-group discussions? How do they approach certain activities and topics?

5) **Involve students in assessment**. Brain research tells us that a great deal of learning occurs when students are asked to evaluate their own work. Plus, having students involved in assessment has some practical benefits for teachers as well. It could mean that the teacher does not have to grade every product but instead can take a more cursory look at some of them (but certainly not all). Here is a great trick that works well with Think-Tac-Toes: (Do not tell the students this up front!) When they have each completed their Think-Tac-Toe products (let's assume for the sake of illustration that they have each completed a total of three), ask each student to pick one product for *you* to evaluate, one for another student to evaluate, and one that they will evaluate themselves. Everyone can use the same assessment tool, such as a rubric or checklist, for the evaluations, but now, instead of having to grade three products from each student, the teacher is grading only

one. In our experience, students are often much harder on themselves than we are when it comes to assigning a grade to their work. It is also a good idea to involve students in the creation of the assessment tool itself. Asking students to design product rubrics and checklists serves two important purposes: 1) It gives them a chance to review information and skills that they have learned, and 2) it helps to ensure that they will meet the evaluation criteria by giving them increased ownership of it.

6) **Don't grade everything**. Usually when we say this to a group of teachers, everyone gasps. This might go against the grain for most professional educators, but, yes, we are suggesting that you resist at times the temptation to formally assess everything that you ask your students to do. You are probably saying to yourself right now, *"If we don't grade it, will they do it?"* Perhaps not. Which is why we do not advise giving an assignment and then telling the students that you will not be grading it. By the time they reach middle school, students have had ample time to figure out how to play the game – and grades are certainly a part of that game. But the fact is that much of what we do with our students ought to be done for practice and preparation for something bigger (perhaps a test or project) and, in that sense, practices really should not be graded. Think back to the sports metaphor we began with in Chapter 1. Practices in sports serve to build skills and confidence. They prepare players for something bigger, a game or match. The same could be said for practice activities in classrooms, and this need for practice can certainly be communicated to students. We certainly believe that teachers should not ask students to complete work that is unnecessary, and we do not want students to think that because we are not grading it, it is not important. But students are capable of understanding that some classroom tasks are building blocks needed for the "bigger picture."

7) **Keep records!** So much of what we learn about students can not be boiled down to a number or a letter. How can we record in a grade book a brilliant comment

or, alternatively, a major gap in thinking? *Qualitative* data is as important as, if not more important than, *quantitative* data. For this reason, we advise coming up with an efficient way to maintain a paper trail of your observations in the classroom and of students' comments. Whether it is a sticky pad that you carry with you at all times, a page of mailing labels that can be added to a file folder later, or a simple pad of paper, you will be glad you have those notes jotted down when report card and parent conference times roll around.

As we envisioned this book, frankly we wrestled with this chapter a bit. Certainly, a topic as important as this one – assessment in a differentiated classroom – could have been the first chapter in this book because, at the end of the day, no assessment process is worth its salt unless we do something with the information it gives us. This is, of course, where the first seven chapters in this book come in to play – the "doing something" part. Differentiating instruction is an on-going cycle of assessing, planning, assessing again, and adjusting until we find the right fit for our students.

Effective differentiation cannot happen without a thoughtful and purposeful approach to assessment.

Differentiated Instruction: Resources

Armstrong, Thomas (2003). *The Multiple Intelligences of Reading and Writing: Making Words Come Alive.*

Bender, William N. (2002). *Differentiating Instruction for Students with Learning Disabilities.*

Benjamin, Amy (2003). *Differentiated Instruction: A Guide for Elementary School Teachers.*

Burke, Kay (1999). *How to Assess Authentic Learning.*

Coil, Carolyn (1997). *Teaching Tools for the 21st Century.*

Coil, Carolyn (2004). *Standards-Based Activities and Assessments for the Differentiated Classroom.*

Heacox, Diane (2002). *Differentiating Instruction in the Regular Classroom: How to Reach and Teach All Learners, Grades 3-12.*

Meador, Karen (2005). *Tiered Activities for Learning Centers: Differentiation in Math, Language Arts, Science & Social Studies.*

Northey, Sheryn S. (2005). *Handbook on Differentiated Instruction for Middle and High Schools.*

Silver, Harvey F., Strong, Richard W., & Perini, Matthew J. (2000). *So Each May Learn: Integrating Learning Styles and Multiple Intelligences.*

Tomlinson, Carol A. (1999). *The Differentiated Classroom: Responding to the Needs of All Learners.*

Tomlinson, Carol A., & Allen, Susan D. (2000). *Leadership for Differentiating Schools & Classrooms.*

Tomlinson, Carol A. (2001). *How to Differentiate Instruction in Mixed-Ability Classrooms.*

Tomlinson, Carol A., & Eidson, Caroline C. (2003). *Differentiation in Practice: A Resource Guide for Differentiating Curriculum, Grades K-5.*

Tomlinson, Carol A., & Eidson, Caroline C. (2003). *Differentiation in Practice: A Resource Guide for Differentiating Curriculum, Grades 5-9.*

Tomlinson, Carol A., & Strickland, Cindy A. (2005). *Differentiation in Practice: A Resource Guide for Differentiating Curriculum, Grades 9-12.*

Winebrenner, Susan (1992). *Teaching Gifted Kids in the Regular Classroom.*

Winebrenner, Susan (1996). *Teaching Kids with Learning Difficulties in the Regular Classroom.*

Wormeli, Rick (2006). *Fair Isn't Always Equal: Assessing & Grading in the Differentiated Classroom.*